THE
WRITER'S
SURVIVAL
GUIDE

THE
WRITER'S
SURVIVAL
GUIDE

RACHEL SIMON

STORY PRESS

CINCINNATI, OHIO

The Writer's Survival Guide. Copyright © 1997 by Rachel Simon. Printed and bound in the United States of America. All rights reserved. No part of this book may be reproduced in any form or by any electronic or mechanical means including information storage and retrieval systems without permission in writing from the publisher, except by a reviewer, who may quote brief passages in a review. Published by Story Press, an imprint of F&W Publications, Inc., 1507 Dana Avenue, Cincinnati, Ohio 45207. (800) 289-0963. First edition.

Story Press Books are available from your local bookstore or direct from the publisher.

01   00   99   98   97   5   4   3   2   1

Library of Congress Cataloging-in-Publication Data

Simon, Rachel.
    The writer's survival guide / Rachel Simon.—1st ed.
        p.   cm.
    Includes index.
    ISBN 1-884910-23-8 (alk. paper)
    1. Authorship—Psychological aspects. 2. Authors—Psychology. 3. Creation (Literary, artistic, etc.) 4. Emotions. I. Title.
PN171.P83S57   1997
808'.02'019—DC20   96-43433
                                                                                        CIP

Designed by Clare Finney
Cover illustration by Helen D'Souza

For Jack Heffron,
whose kindness helped me see through,
and for Deborah Cors,
facilitator of phoenixes

CONTENTS

PART I: THE BASICS

PART II: THE PROCESS

INTRODUCTION

I was seven when I decided to be a writer. My moment of revelation came when I was lying on the sofa in our dining room, curled beside my mother as she took her afternoon nap and I, supposedly, napped too. But instead of sleeping, I occupied myself with my usual antinap activity, which consisted of trying to create pictures out of the cracked paint in the ceiling while I contemplated my future. I had long since tired of grown-ups asking, "And what are you going to be when you grow up?" Many were the arbitrary replies I had given: ballerina, teacher, mommy. But I knew in my heart that none of these was true, so I struggled to come up with a more genuine response. That afternoon, as the sun settled on top of us and the house sighed deeper into its foundation, the answer finally came to me: *Aha! I'll be a writer!* Somehow I knew—in spite of having written nothing but alphabet exercises so far in my life—that this was not a lie.

I thought, *I can do that.*

But I had no idea what it meant to be a writer. I imagined it meant *writing*, pure and simple. You came up with stories, penciled them down, and then, after passing through several magic chambers, perhaps drinking a secret potion or two along the way, you found those words bound together into a book. People bought and read the book, and then you wrote another.

I began with stories and over the years added correspondence, journal writing, poetry, lyrics, and novels. I loved coming up with narratives, transcribing dialogue from my mind to the page, making my friends giggle or grow plaintive after reading my work. So what if I wasn't a blonde knockout or a swift-footed Mercury at the hundred-yard dash? If all my piecrusts in Home Ec flaked like aged plaster and my sculptures in Art class were so asymmetrical they kept tipping over and shattering on the linoleum? I could do something that I enjoyed enormously and everyone else respected: I could write.

But as biology extruded me from childhood into adolescence, and I discovered self-consciousness, I began to suspect that I didn't actually know what it meant to be a writer. Clearly, it meant more than penciling drafts into spiral notebooks. It also meant submitting work for acceptance, and the deeper the inevitability of submission drilled itself into me, the more my dread erupted. I just couldn't imagine sending my work away to a publisher. They (and it was an amorphous, mysterious *they*, vaguely resembling the panel of angels—or was it judges?—at the gates to the great Hereafter) knew so much more than I did. My work couldn't possibly be good enough for them. I could never measure up. As if that fear weren't crippling enough, I realized—after a high school teacher critiqued some of my stories, sitting me down for hours in the dining hall one day and gently pointing out where I could edit each—that being a writer meant working hard, harder than I'd thought. It also meant admitting that my stories might be flawed or, as I put it to myself, "wrong"—that my cinematic references were too obscure to be useful, that my tendency to be unspecific about my narrator's gender was confusing to the reader, that the words I used to describe the schizophrenic hippie candlemaker were more intellectual than a hippie voice should allow.

So something was "wrong" with my stories. "I understand," I muttered to the teacher, slouching with embarrassment, gulping back my shame, because at that very moment, I was making the fatal leap: Having something wrong with my work, I erroneously thought, meant admitting that something was wrong with *me*. Egregiously wrong. Wronger than anyone else's wrong, particularly anyone bold (and talented!) enough to call herself a writer. Wrong enough to quit.

So I quit. Clearly, I wasn't worthy of being a writer.

And for six years I did not scribble another piece of fiction.

I now know that this writer's block, as with all writer's blocks, was also connected to my self-image, which was undergoing seismic upheaval at the time. But my fears about being a writer were genuine and, as I would later discover, similar to fears felt by all writers in the early stages of their development: *I can't, ergo I'm not, ergo I shouldn't.*

Only years later, after I returned to writing, did I come to understand that being a writer means much more than putting words on a page. Being a writer means pushing yourself up against your emotional limits, and then pushing through. Being a writer means confronting your psychological shortcomings, and continuing in spite of them. Being a writer means continually facing hoops of fire— everything you feel about yourself and think about the world—and, after a moment to assess them and determine the angle of your trajectory, launching yourself through, maintaining the faith that you will land safely.

This lesson took me years to see. And it has only been reinforced as I have become a professional writer and teacher:

The biggest impediment to writing is not friends or teachers or editors or anything else external. Not the other stars in the classroom, nor your eye-rolling wife, nor the denouement that won't get done, nor even the editor who wouldn't buy or promote your book. The biggest impediment to writing is you.

That means your emotions, your beliefs, your defense mechanisms, your conflicts, your self-image, your ability to handle practical decisions, and everything else that goes into making you believe you can't, or aren't, or shouldn't.

Indeed, being a writer means experiencing the whole emotional shebang, from misery to bliss, and becoming intimate with every emotion—the good, the bad, and the glorious. And it means coping with all the associated dilemmas of a writing life, from how to make time when it means you have to say no to your loved ones, to how to remain productive when your best story keeps getting rejected, to how to decide whether to enter a writing program when you're too scared, to how to support yourself as a writer when you don't have a trust fund.

In all my years of writing and teaching, I've seen many talented writers throw in the towel, and seldom is their discontinuance due to an impasse with craft or even the publishing industry. Standards we can teach ourselves, technique we can practice, and publishing troubles don't necessarily cause the ink in our pens to dry.

Instead, when writers stop writing, it is almost always because of such things as competitiveness with talented others who are sharing not just the workshop table but also the admiration of the teacher; envy toward more prolific authors whose dust jackets simply must bear the subliminal message *Buy me*; frustration that our exquisitely original voice keeps mating itself to lackluster, clichéd narratives and endings that fizzle; shame over taking *three whole months* on a story when our co-workers keep saying, "It's not done *yet?*"; paranoia over Uncle Merv's withdrawing the invitation to Thanksgiving after he recognizes that he was the model for the nefarious clockmaker with the cackle and downy mole.

This book was written to help writers live the writing life and understand what that means. By weaving my own stories with the stories of others, I present the whole writerly journey—what writers can expect to feel, when in the process they can expect to feel it, and specific advice on how they might make all their emotions work for them, whether those emotions are positive or negative. I also present all the major practical decisions writers have to make—from setting up when and where to write, to deciding how to educate oneself, to handling criticism—and again, I offer specific advice.

The book is set up to be read straight through and then used as a handy reference tool. It is meant to be marked up, coffee stained, highlighted, and dog-eared—i.e., it is meant to be used, and writers will be encouraged to use it. It is as much a book of inspiration as it is a book of solution.

The goal is twofold. First, it is to provide beginning writers with an emotional and practical map that will help them recognize and handle competitiveness, frustration, euphoria, etc., and recognize and handle the many practical decisions they must make. Second, the goal is to provide experienced writers with a comforting and thoughtful place that will help them diagnose any case of the blues, "prescribe" remedies they might need, and guide them through major decisions. The overall goal is to show writers, whether beginning or advanced, many ways to keep going.

Part I, "The Basics," focuses on the fundamental emotional, philosophical, and logistical issues that beset all writers, from novice to Nobel Prize laureate. Part II, "The Process," breaks down the act of writing into four categories—long-term preparation, or "Education"; shorter-term preparation, or "Before the Draft"; the writing experience itself, "During the Draft"; and writer's block, or "When You're Stuck"—elaborating on the emotional highs and lows and practical predicaments of each. Part III, "Becoming an Author," describes what happens to writers' emotions and what dilemmas writers must face as they enter the publishing world and achieve success.

All writers need a good friend with whom they can share their fervor, and who will believe in them. Not all writers are fortunate enough to have such a friend. I hope this book will fill the gap so when you feel alone, wrestling with the fears you believe no writer has felt before, you can open these pages and realize that no obstacle is too formidable. Maybe then you won't have to struggle as much and can devote your time to craft, and imagination, and simply having *fun*.

PART ONE

THE BASICS

CHAPTER ONE

THE BIG QUESTIONS

I teach private classes in writing, one-on-one tutorials in which the entire course is tailored to the needs of that individual student.

I always imagine, before I meet with students for the first time, that their big questions will concern technique. How can I make my characters more distinct? Is there a better way to handle the structure of this piece?

Such questions *are* usually the basis of our first meeting or two.

But inevitably, by the third or fourth meeting, those questions taper off, and in their place spring up different questions. These new queries lurk beneath all the others, poking up from time to time to jolt the writer into self-examination or self-doubt or, sometimes, paralysis. They are, more than characterization or narrative technique, what the writer really wants to know:

Why should I—or anyone—write?

Do I have talent, and how can I tell?

How big a commitment can (or should) I make?

These concerns are almost invariably in the minds of every writer. I have heard them from people so new to writing they never kept a journal before our classes and from people who had published in prestigious magazines and won major literary awards. Regardless of the source, when these questions first emerge in class, it is almost always subtly, perhaps even imperceptibly, like a mumbled *Gesundheit* or a comment about the weather. Seldom does the student break eye contact; these questions are so trivial, they are not even speed bumps in our class. Or so the student would like me to believe.

But I know better. We (and I say "we" because of course I have been needled by the same issues) ask these questions when we fear we aren't good enough. We think that there must be "right" answers to these questions, and since we don't know them, we shouldn't really continue writing. We must be deluding ourselves. We are impostors.

I've come to suspect that many writers were born into families where they were rarely praised. Perhaps their needs were ignored or minimized while the parents battered their way through their own lives. Or perhaps the parents were excessively demanding, holding out some delicious prize, telling the future writer, "Jump! Higher!" while always raising or hiding the prize, ensuring that success could never be achieved. I have even met writers who spent their childhoods being blatantly ridiculed by the people they most respected.

Consequently, many people begin writing with a profound lack of faith in themselves. They might even be wrestling with depression. They know they want to write; maybe they even *like* writing. But deep down, they don't feel worthy of writing. It seems so venerable, so important. How could they—measly little they, surely not as resolute and articulate and gifted as any writer they could buy in the airport, much less a Faulkner or a Fitzgerald—grant themselves the permission to go for it?

So they come to me with their souls open. They have been hurting for so long with their secret feelings of inadequacy that they are now aching for reassurance.

I address this by going through each of the big questions, and usually, by the time I'm finished, they feel a little better.

WHY SHOULD I—OR ANYONE—WRITE?

There are no correct reasons to write. We just think there are. We read so many interviews with writers that we get the sense that those who have "made it" must know the way to do it—and that there is, indeed, one way. This is because we forget that writing is not a formula; we think, "Since he succeeded by writing on a laptop computer from four to six in the morning before work, I will succeed by doing the same." So when writers tell interviewers that they write because they have something to say about "the human condition," or because they escaped a prison in a third world country and want to expose political cruelty, or because they have a young daughter and like to make her laugh with their stories, we think these should be our answers, too. And woe be unto us if we realize that that is not so.

In all my years of writing and teaching writing, I have heard hundreds of reasons for why people write, but the most compelling one, the one that seems at the core of the most persistent (and usually successful) writers, is that they write because they like to write. Like eating a pizza or splashing in the ocean or savoring a four-minute kiss with a new lover, these writers write because *it feels good.*

This does not remotely mean that they don't grapple with characters or language. It doesn't necessarily mean that they have a jolly old time every day they sit down to write. It certainly doesn't mean that they exist in an aura of unrelenting inspiration.

Rather, when writing feels good it means that something, at some point in the process, lights up inside them. This feeling might come through the Zen-like serenity found in hard work, or the simple satisfaction of gliding a ballpoint pen along a white page, or the wonder of seeing something blossom where previously there had been nothing, or the worldly revelations encountered during exploration of thematic material, or the psychic *ping!* that echoes after two disparate elements connect into a shockingly perfect metaphor, or the delight that permeates as some latent humor snake-charms up from the page, or the tender gratification that carries us through the day after we wring our own heart into tears. It can come in a million ways. But as long as it comes, the writer almost always keeps writing.

What about those other reasons, the ones we hear about but that may not seem to apply to us? I write because I:

have something to say

like to read

want to stick it to my dictator/boss/ex-husband/mother

lived a fascinating life I want to document

want to make a lot of money

want to see my name in print

must

All of these—and many other reasons—might well be valid incentives to start us on the path to being a writer. Anything could serve that role: being bored on a Saturday afternoon, taking a writing class because our best friend is taking it too, proving ourselves to all those who have ever kicked sand in our faces. But the reasons why we start and the reasons why we continue are seldom the same.

Years ago, I read a book on meditation that said there are two obstacles to enlightenment: beginning and continuing. It takes a certain confluence of enthusiasm and motivation to embark on the long journey of meditation. Then, after the novice meditator has acquired technique, it takes a whole new shade of enthusiasm and a whole new set of motivations to stay the course.

This is equally true of marriage, or studying for a Ph.D., or playing the violin, or learning classical Latin. We start for one reason; we keep going for others.

All reasons are valid for starting to write. But the one reason that will keep you going is that somehow—in ways you may or may not be able to identify—it makes you feel good.

Occasionally, this answer seems too simple for some students. Yes, they admit, writing makes them feel good, but . . . but . . . there must be more to it. How can feeling good be enough of a reason to do anything?

This is always where I realize that the student is not asking me for the correct *Why* at all. The student is asking me for permission to do something just to *do* it.

From the day we were born, we were taught that all activities that feel good come with a price. Roses smell lovely but pick one and you'll get thorns in your fingers. Chocolate chip cookies taste like a sugar Eden but eat all you want and you'll get cavities. Champagne brings hangovers; fireplaces bring pollution; sunbathing brings cancer; lovemaking brings STDs or heartbreak.

Or, as watercooler wisdom would have it, if it feels good, it's got to be bad for you.

We do admit that there are a few exceptions. Sleeping, for instance. Stepping into a hot shower. Hugging our children. Laughing with friends. Drinking an icy glass of water on a hot day. With such activities, we tell ourselves, "This will feel good. For that reason alone, I will do it." We give ourselves permission.

The same is required of writing. If it makes you feel good, that is enough reason to keep going.

You might have been taught that every silver lining comes with a cloud, but that doesn't mean you have to live in fear of clouds. Let other people be martyrs and submit to lives devoid of fun. Writing won't do you wrong; it won't prick your fingers, pad your dentist's retirement fund, cause cotton mouth, provoke the ire of the EPA, invite melanoma, or make you need penicillin or Prozac. Writing will only get you more connected to yourself and to the world. It feels good because it is one of the best ways, short of dreaming or having a shamanistic experience, to explore your soul.

That is, writing doesn't only feel good. Writing is also good *for* you.

And when we have that kind of opportunity, which so few people have, we would be remiss to avoid it. It is a gift of pleasure. Other people envy us because they don't have it; they see it as a privilege, the way we get the big picture while escaping the same tedium that might enmesh them and thumb our nose at the same traumas that might debilitate them. And they are right. We may contend with the drudgeries of the everyday, and we certainly may get black and blue from the fisticuffs of life, but we do so while knowing there is more. We know we can spy into our own minds and discover not just the familiar creepy basements and closets jammed with skeletons, but also grand halls of beauty, whole wings of understanding, secret passageways between the past and the present, and fragrant terraced gardens that sprawl on forever. We know that the deeper we look into ourselves, the more generously we can view the world. And we *want* to look. Because we have learned that such exploration is enjoyable and such examination gratifying, and revelation—when it occurs, which it will when you're writing, at least occasionally, maybe even frequently—is 100 percent delight.

So whenever the *Why* question begins to creep back in, tell yourself that it's just you doubting that you are worthy of pleasure. And then tell yourself that a life without pleasure is merely a life. A life *with* pleasure can be a glory.

DO I HAVE TALENT, AND HOW CAN I TELL?

We worry, and compare ourselves. We sit in our writing classes or libraries and gaze out at others while a little virus of doubt ululates in our heads: *She* has talent because she writes so easily; *he* has talent because he produces a story a week; *they* have talent because they have achieved the nirvana of publication. Look at them all—born with *talent*. But alas, that seems not to be our fate. We bemoan how writing is hard work for us; we're lucky to turn out about a story a year; we'll never get into *The New Yorker*. Like height and hair color, talent must be in the genes, and how can we fight biology? We may be able to strap on high heels and Clairol our hair, but when it comes to writing, we will simply never give ourselves what our DNA did not.

I have heard this lament from almost every writer I have ever known, or else I hear the opposite: I have talent, and therefore I will succeed, whether or not I ever sit down to write.

The concept of talent acts almost as a military checkpoint inside us. Those who think they might have it allow themselves to pass through and continue. Those who don't turn back, dejected.

I am fully aware of the power of this word. Although I wrote throughout my childhood, I entered a major writer's block at eighteen and did not recover until I was twenty-four. I re-began with sentences, worked my way up to paragraphs, and finally graduated to stories. Soon thereafter, I began taking a writing class. Right after the first session, I intensified my pace, trying to produce a story a week so I'd have something new to read each time we met. Often my work elicited excited comments from my classmates, but I wanted something *more*, though I wasn't sure what. After my third or fourth story, I found out. My teacher let my fellow students share their assessments of the piece, and then, when it was her turn, she announced to me, the class—the whole goddamn world!—"Rachel has talent."

This was ambrosia. An acceptance to Harvard and a gold star from the Pulitzer committee. I levitated for days. And wrote harder. Now I *knew* something. Now my fire burned higher.

Only years later did I realize how influential that teacher's words had been, and how silly I was to have put such stock in them. I was already writing diligently and daily. I was already writing not because I "had talent," but because I wanted to write. Hearing my teacher's declaration of my talent kicked me a little harder and ratcheted up my confidence a notch or two, but I think it also made me believe in the concept of talent—a concept of which I have become increasingly dubious.

What *is* talent? I have seen writers who couldn't cobble together a coherent sentence, whose work was so bad it set classes into symphonies of eeks and groans—and who, five years later, were publishing their first book. I have also seen writers who created masterpieces of creative vision in writing class, who seemed destined for some pantheon of Great Twentieth Century Authors—and who, when class ended, never typed anything but space breaks again. The former writers gave the appearance of having no talent, yet they succeeded. The latter writers seemed to have prodigious talent, yet they failed.

Does that mean both kinds of writers defied biology? Or that talent has nothing to do with genes?

My dictionary provides a reassuring answer. Talent, it says, is a "natural readiness in learning and doing in a particular field; an inborn resource that may or may not be developed."

I like this definition, because it suggests that talent is like a nest in which we can choose to grow—or choose to wither. In other words, this definition refers to potential, not actuality; to choice, not inevitability.

Talent is not *You Are Here*. Talent is *You Can Get Here If You Try*.

When we ask ourselves if we have talent, we are asking the wrong question. Success is not predetermined. Some people may write more easily than others, or more prolifically, or with greater acknowledgment by the outside world, but if they don't really yearn to keep going and achieve greater and greater levels of improvement with their work, they will never achieve their potential.

If you're working harder than you think possible, and want to keep getting better, and you can admit your imperfections so you can keep learning, and you are willing to go the long haul, then you have talent. Whether that means you are cultivating some mysterious, biological force that was already within you or you are planting a force that wasn't there does not matter.

In other words, the issue is not talent. The issue is passion. If you have it, you'll keep moving onward and upward, regardless of whether any teacher has told you that you have talent. If you don't have passion, you'll fizzle out, regardless of whether any teacher once proclaimed you a prodigy.

The designation doesn't matter. Only the desire does.

HOW BIG A COMMITMENT CAN (OR SHOULD) I MAKE?

Writing is not unlike marriage; the more assiduously you work at it, the better the results will be. Sometimes it's a demanding chore to keep up the optimism and energy, and you pout or complain or forget why you wanted this in the first place. But usually over the years it becomes clear that your efforts are worthwhile and have in fact led to unimaginable rewards. Then you can continue more avidly than ever, richer in faith and conviction, guided by wisdom.

Unlike marital commitments, though, we have no socially pre-
scribed rules of behavior for writing commitments. We see no billboard displays of authors embracing their beloved keyboards.
Television programs broadcast no implied messages about the most
revered or reviled degrees of literary devotion. Rock songs never address the consistency with which we must maintain our writing fi-
delity. We are on our own to figure out the rules.

Or to realize there are no rules, except for the ones we make for
ourselves.

So how big a commitment can and should we make?

First of all, we need to recognize that commitment is directly re-
lated to the permission and passion I discussed above. Inevitably,
people who cannot give themselves permission to do what feels good
and people who sustain no passion for writing are unable to make a
writing commitment at all. Both kinds of people include students
who withdraw from class or beginning writers who abandon their
newly devised writing regimen after the first month or so. That
quickly, they realize that writing means sitting down and doing it—
and, as a result, not sewing on a button, or going fishing, or taking
a second job, or hanging out after aerobics class at the gym, or attending the theater. They discover they don't want to spend their
time on something that does not give immediate payback in terms
of errands completed or money in the bank, or else they realize they
love other aspects of life more than they love writing. Either way, the
seesaw of writing versus real life has clearly thudded down on the
side of real life. Their options are not in doubt: They can't or don't
want to do it, and they quit.

Then there are the people who can allow themselves permission
some of the time and who feel not a passion but a fondness for writing.
These people make a moderate commitment. They are writers who
occasionally produce complete pieces of fiction—but only when they
aren't interrupting their writing to help out their boss, or volunteer
for a neighborhood organization. The seesaw rocks near a balanced
position but since their options seem so broad, they sometimes dip
into doubt and not-writing. If they are students, they stay in classes
to feel they are writing. If they are not students, they tend to get into
a cycle of falling off and climbing back onto the horse. Often they
do make substantial progress over time, but since they break up their

writing routine so regularly, they sometimes grow frustrated that they are not improving more rapidly.

Finally, there are people who so love to do what feels good and so love writing that they want to hop into bed with writing and spend the rest of their existence caressing it. These are the writers who write every day for hours, whose imagination, even when they leave the desk, orbits them like a long-lasting cologne, who use every twig on the ground and clank on the street and scent in the air as a trigger for their memories and ideas, who constantly ponder the connections between what they are living and what they are writing. Their seesaw slammed down toward writing, and they never want to kick it back up.

We make the commitment our hearts tell us to make, and that is all we *should* do. If you grant yourself permission to write, and you revel in the process of writing, and you long to become a great writer, and you want to get published, then give it your all. For tips on time management, see chapter four, "The Big (and Small) Logistics." If, however, you give yourself more permission to play in your jazz trio, or to go shopping, or to engage in other nonwriting activities than you give yourself to write, and if your feelings toward writing fall more into the category of "Eh, it's okay" than into the category of love, and if you wouldn't beg, bargain, and steal from any number of supernatural powers to learn the secrets of honing your unique voice, and if you truly, honestly are unmoved about the thought of getting published, then it's fine to write more erratically—as long as you can accept that that may cause your dreams of being an author to switch onto a slower track.

There are no rules. All that matters is that you can live with yourself, however intensively or lightly you make your commitment.

But what about straying from the commitment? Students ask me this all the time. They're cooking along for several weeks, maybe even months, and then *boom!* They butt up against the arrival of a new baby, or their church choir's trip to Vienna, or a friend's severe illness. And while their commitment to writing doesn't alter, the amount of writing they can actually *do* wanes.

Sometimes they fret. They come to me as if I am their confessor and, head down, eyes brimming with contrition, admit that they didn't put in much time this week. They expect me to pronounce some judgment on them. They tell me they must not really be a writer, that they were just lucky to do what they'd done before, that they've used it all up.

I tell them that commitment is an overall decision that we can't always express actively. In marriage, we're expected to be fully present every day. But in writing, we can occasionally step out. Circumstances keep us from getting to our literary bed. Moods seduce us. We must—or want to—do other things.

When I was creating my first novel, I wrote eight, ten, sometimes twelve hours a day. To avoid leaving the library where I was scribbling my first draft, I snuck some doughy, soundless lunch into the building every morning and ate it surreptitiously in the stacks in the afternoon. To avoid breaking my writing trance when I was typing up the draft at home, I napped at my computer and learned to talk to myself. I took no days off, not even half-days. I didn't answer phone calls, sending postcards to friends asking for their understanding. I was so committed that near the end I barely laundered my clothes.

I've also had times in my life when other aspects of living were far more important than writing. The first few months of a new romance, when all I wanted to do was float in the heat and mind of a new person. The few months before and after my books' publications, when all I wanted to do was give readings and signings. And the occasional months of blues, when all I wanted to do was brood, sleep, read the paper, and wait it out.

During all those periods, I stepped away from most of my writing, except for journal writing.

But whether I'm writing fiction with vigor or not writing it at all, I am clear on my commitment. Sometimes it is realized; sometimes it is inactive. I don't worry about the latter, because I know I will return to my usual high level of commitment, and because I know that we periodically need to toggle ourselves from output to input mode, just so we have more thematic and narrative inspiration to boost our work to a new level.

Make no apologies if you take a break. Breaks can be helpful, and they don't mean you aren't committed.

Worry only if you find you take more breaks than not, if you use real life as an excuse to vacillate on your commitment. If that happens, ask yourself if you really *are* committed. That is, ask if you give yourself permission to write, if you feel a passion for writing, how much you want to master the craft, and how earnestly you long to be published.

If your answers have changed from what they originally were, then reassess your commitment. If they are the same answers but your efforts have disappeared, then examine the possibility that your true feelings have changed and you need to admit that to yourself.

As with talent, the question to ask about commitment is not about commitment per se, but how much writing means to us, and how much we truly—once we know what that means—want to have writing in our lives.

CHAPTER TWO

THE BIG EMOTIONS AND STATES OF MIND

Every writer who writes long enough will experience each of these emotions and states of mind. Sometimes they bedevil us; sometimes they inspire us. But there is no avoiding them, regardless of who we are.

This chapter describes how to recognize each emotion and state of mind. The next chapter suggests general approaches for handling the harder ones.

Competitiveness: A seething desire to best everyone else. Sometimes the competition pool is immediately around us: the people in our writing group or class. Sometimes it is as immense as the entire literary world. In either case, we believe that all the writers in our imaginary pool—including us—are being rated by a single panel of judges, and so we compare ourselves along the same scale as those in our pool, searching for the drooping smile or sloppy finish that will rate our competitors as less than a perfect 10. We write harder to prove we are better. On rare occasions, we consider sabotage or delight when our primary rival screws up in the eyes of those we want to please.

An interviewer once told me that most writers are second born (as am I) or were in some other way raised in a position of competitiveness with others. Perhaps the rival was mom's boyfriend, and the territory at stake was mom's affection. Perhaps the rival was the other smartest kid in the class. In any event, we learned early that, to get to the top, we had to win out over others during our climb up. And we wanted to be on top, because that, we believed, was the way we would finally feel good about ourselves and earn specialness, love, and the kindness of others.

Competitiveness is something we feel throughout our writing careers. No writer seems immune. I recently learned from Sophy Burnham's book *For Writers Only* that Robert Frost, while attending a poetry reading by Robert Lowell, was so unable to tolerate the attention going to another poet that he actually set a fire in the back of the auditorium. This may not have given Frost the adoration he desired, but it certainly diverted the audience's attention from Lowell.

We must decide whether to make competitiveness our foe or friend. If it is allowed to run unbridled, it will consume us with hatred for others. It will prod us toward bitterness and sarcasm, incite us to commit undignified acts, drain the words "Congratulations!" "Well done!" and "you" from our vocabulary, shrivel us into the kind of person about whom others whisper, "She is not generous in spirit; we don't want to be like her." Competitiveness unchecked makes us ruthless and emotionally ugly, turning us into literary Dorian Grays.

If competitiveness is harnessed, though, we see others not as rivals but as examples of what we too can be. For instance, our friend's book sold 100,000 copies and ours only 2,000. We can snivel and gripe, or we can embark on a research project to understand why the public liked his book so much more than ours. Perhaps we find there is a greater difference between publishers than we had previously thought, and so we discover we need to become more alert to the strengths and goals of each house. Or perhaps we find that our friend wrote on a subject that, we now see, is enormously popular, and so we can explore whether we want to write about a similar or equally popular subject ourselves.

Competitiveness can spur us to work more diligently and become more resourceful. It can steer us toward determination, self-reliance, and more insight, not more rancor. Our "rival" really wants the same support and accolades that we do. Hence, competitiveness properly appreciated can infuse our vocabulary with genuine expressions of praise for others, metamorphose us into the kind of person about whom others exclaim, "She is bighearted, a torch who lights our path." It can make us noble and emotionally attractive, transforming us as Scrooge was transformed after he awoke on Christmas day.

One danger in utilizing competitiveness, however, cannot be overlooked. Many is the beginning writer who turns his feelings of competitiveness into a quest for self-improvement—but does so by making his own work into an imitation of his competitor's. That is, he takes what made his work original and shovels it out the door, then warps and molds what remains into a form already created by someone else. He is not really pursuing self-improvement as much as he is avoiding fear.

I did this with several successful literary writers when I was younger and wound up producing stories that were devoid of my own vision. I remember showing one such story to a teacher. "But it doesn't work," she said, holding the limp manuscript in her hand. I looked at her in defensiveness and sorrow. "It works for Alice Munro," I asserted. "Yes," she said, slapping down the pages. "But you're not Alice Munro. You're Rachel Simon."

In other words, we need to use competitiveness, but we cannot let competitiveness bully us into forgetting that we are still ourselves: unique individuals. Sometimes it will tempt us to move in directions where we don't want to go—or where, given our writerly dispositions, we should *not* go. We must evaluate this and so choose our lessons wisely. Be willing to venture into new realms and then return home if necessary. Establish whatever boundaries are required. Give ourselves the patience to experiment and learn. (See "Boundaries" and "Patience" in chapter three.)

Competitiveness is a fine guide to lead us into adventure. We just need to parent ourselves a bit so we take risks without risking amnesia.

Confidence: A calm hum of faith in ourselves. Though we may have been confident about other aspects of our lives before we began writing, confidence on the page comes only through experience: the short story worked to an incandescent climax, the novel painstakingly refined. Confidence is an emotion we acquire through the evidence—to ourselves—of our own unflagging competence. It arrives in dribbles at first but eventually, after we've written for a long time, solidifies into a consistent self-assurance that is virtually unshakable and that transcends the hours at the desk to bolster us through all other aspects of our day.

Some writers, when beginning their careers, feel the need to affect a public persona of absolute confidence. Usually these people have done much more dreaming than writing and so are quite unfamiliar with the hard work involved. Often they discuss their stories and boast about the spectacular flight path of their soon-to-be careers before they've written a word, trying to impress the world with their brilliance. Other beginning writers who are already in the trenches sometimes allow such seemingly confident people to deter them; "I'll never find it that easy," they mope, occasionally falling into writer's block. But in fact these boasters are cocky—perhaps to the point of arrogance—not confident. They are more focused on what others think of them than on how rigorously they can push themselves to improve. Sometimes, when they face the daily pondering and solitude and realize that public adoration is only a minuscule part of writing, they shed their false confidence, achieve a level of humility, and get to work. Otherwise, they quit.

Confidence in writing takes years and a great deal of labor. It is earned, like wrinkles or trust.

Confidence in writing also has less to do with external validation than we believe. External validation certainly has its place: A teacher's hurrah can rouse us to write harder, an editor's acceptance letter can motivate us to submit more. But external validation inspires action and eagerness; external validation does not confidence make. A much-published author may have little confidence, a barely published author may have a lot. My least confident student is the one who has won the most notable awards, whose stories have appeared in the most prestigious magazines. She continually falls into writer's block, so lacking in self-belief is she. My most confident student is the one who has not published yet, but who writes every day, growing more confident as he watches his work develop.

Confidence in writing comes from writing and writing and writing while striving consistently to improve. An acceptance from a publisher may flambé our confidence, but it does not serve up the original treat. That we must do ourselves. An acceptance gives a momentary high that can burn out quickly. Only hard work and betterment lead to the long-lasting, deep feeling of confidence.

Contemplativeness: A peaceful, prolonged, and leisurely musing. This is a slowing down of thought to which we retrain ourselves; instead of mentally careening toward our destination, we let ourselves stroll, checking out all the cobwebbed alleys and crooked doorways and leaded windows on our way there, leaving ourselves open to taking new paths. Contemplativeness is a slow, midnight simmer in a luxurious bubble bath, not a zippy shower timed to end just as the coffee has brewed. It is a quiet meandering. An "Ah!" that feels like "Aaaaahhhhh." It is revelation by way of relaxation.

Federal Express ads raise our pulse. MTV slices our concentration into nanoseconds. Our remote control plays tag with fifty storylines. We fax, we phone, we Internet. Our families say, "When are you going to get published already?" We think we should be further along with our writing lives. When we sit down to write, a locomotive hurtles through our minds. *Now! Fast! Faster, you procrastinating idiot! It shouldn't take this long! Only numskulls take this long! Macht schnell! Mush!* We barrel through our words and characters as if we have actual deadlines—"By June, I'll have five stories done"; "By my fortieth birthday, I'll have sold a book"—and if we don't meet them, we expect some literary Judgment Day to shuttle us directly to Hell.

Contemplativeness comes only after we have dispensed with such high-speed expectations by realizing that the expectations themselves slow us down. Urgency zeroes in on the finish line, not on words and characters and structure and metaphors and secondary themes. So we get sloppy, empty stories, if we get any stories at all. Nothing we feel our way through, let alone feel good about. Consequently, we *can't* make our goals. In addition, we see writing as a chore, eliminating all possibility of fun.

Contemplativeness does not come in a first draft. It comes during revision, when we slide so deeply into the text that our breathing slows. It comes when we sit with an image or character trait or scene and carefully sculpt it, taking as long to complete the task as is required—which is undoubtedly much longer than our urgent self would have allowed us. We don't rip a cake out of the oven just because we feel like eating it this very moment. We wait until it has cooked. We know baking takes time and control our salivary glands accordingly.

One of the great benefits of writing, contemplativeness stays with us throughout the rest of our days, enabling us to make calm, informed decisions about the real people around us as well as the imaginary people inside us. It gives a poise and groundedness to our personal style, replaces our impulsiveness with studied insight, endows our opinions with certainty. It provides us with a quiet balcony from which we can ponder the world.

Ego: A rigid self-perception of supposed perfection. Ego is as stiff and stubborn as prison bars, with which—if we're lucky—we ultimately realize it has much in common. We must be perfect. We must ensure that others see us as perfect, too. We long for people to perceive us as notable, and dazzling, and original, and masterful because we fear that if they don't, they, and we, will realize that in fact we are not notable, dazzling, original, masterful. And if we realize *that*, then we fear that everything we believe will fall apart; we will crumble and blow away, a nothing suddenly exposed to the world as a nothing.

Ego is not self-esteem, though we often use the words synonymously. Self-esteem is a good opinion of oneself, a view of oneself as worthy, a consistent flow of self-respect. Ego (in the nonFreudian way I am using it here) is more focused on self-importance, usually to the point of vanity. A healthy self-esteem is not punctured by others' comments about our work, but those same comments may make our ego hop about in fury. Self-esteem is necessary in writing and in life, because it enables us to dream and to try. Ego—that self-conscious sense that we are distinct from and usually better than others—only gets in our way, because it focuses on us and the laurels our work will give us, not on the process, not on the work.

All beginning and some advanced writers place a high value on ego. *I can do it, no problem. I am special, so I don't need to work as hard as others. I wrote it; therefore, it's good.* We get so caught up in how the writing reflects our personalities that we can't let our work be perceived as flawed. If *it* is flawed, *we* are flawed. Which means, in practice, that we receive critiques in one of two ways: We lash out at the messenger for giving us such ill-conceived or (we think) malicious appraisals, or we flagellate ourselves for being stupid and doing shoddy work. Either way, we work no more on the piece.

Ego rears its head most when we think a piece is complete and find out, whether through the comments of others or by ourselves, that the piece still needs work. We become defensive. "I spent a whole week on that story, and if it's not done, well then I just don't care!" Or, "But it really happened that way!" Or, "Oh, stop being so nitpicky; I can get away with it." Our ego can't allow us to slow down and go back into the piece. It obstructs process with the steadfastness of General Patton. Our ego suspects that if it doesn't resist more work, its very existence will be threatened.

For assistance in countering the effects of ego, refer to "Humility" and "Patience" in chapter three, and "Handling Criticism" in chapter seven. Also, bear in mind this most important of points: When we read books, our primary concern is to slip fully out of our own lives and get sucked into what novelist John Gardner calls the fictional dream created by the writer. Our primary concern is *not* to dwell upon whether or not the writer is a genius. Certainly, the writer is important as the creator who hatched and nurtured this world. But if the writer's ego has prevented her from working as hard as she could—refining the language, discerning the best pacing—we will find ourselves yanked out of the fictional dream. Then we won't care about the writer and may even dislike her. Certainly we will be unlikely to read her again. All writers striving to reduce their ego must never forget this most essential fact.

Ego is one of the biggest enemies a writer ever encounters. It is the parent of laziness, the sibling of pride, the spouse of shame. It makes us bitter about others' successes and too paralyzed to keep trying. We cannot fully enter the tournament of writing until we have stripped away our ego. If we don't, we will never persist long enough to achieve confidence or meaningfulness, much less euphoria.

Energy: A sustained capacity for and love of vigor. We feel energy when we've been writing with such concentration and the work is going so smoothly that we forget lunch, the day of the week, our own names. We rise from the desk, mentally foggy yet almost perversely charged up. The writing has excited all our molecules. We are bubbling inside. We are making associations and insights with electric ease. We have eaten our literary spinach, and our minds are more potent than ever.

But the expression of energy is seldom immediate. After a session of writing, we are often spent, our mouths unhinged, our eyes pooling. We stumble back to reality, our spoken sentences unraveling somewhere in the predicate. We apologize for being dull. Only when time has passed—a few hours' rest, a night's sleep—does energy seize us. Then, it propels us much farther than we would have gone otherwise. We taste new colors and smell shifting hues. We understand the most subtle of nuances. We've had a workover and now we're ready for the party. We might even have physical strengths we've never had before.

In addition, energy is cumulative. While we may feel a noticeable surge of energy after a single session at the desk, the amount we feel after months of consistent writing is astounding. We become pinballs, bouncing into everything, always excited, eyes sparkling. The world is our teacher, and we want to learn all. People ask, "What's happened to you? You seem so alive!" They wonder if we're in love, or on some new drug or diet.

Part of why writing leads to energy is that it reacquaints us with hope. Not only are we practicing the mental acrobatics we have studied at our desks, but we are reveling in the sense that things will work out: The story will come to a striking climax, the revision will erase whole chapters of text while giving rise to new ones, the piece will sell. And since we are clicking along on hope when we face the paper, we continue when we face our personnel director, or spouse, or children. Everything seems lit in a rosier light. We have faith. We want to dance.

Envy: A punch of rage when someone else has what you do not. Envy strikes suddenly, a flash reaction to some provocation. This could be the moment we realize, as a friend is reading us a story that is so much more skillfully composed than any we have ever considered writing, that she is more developed than we. Or it could be the second we hear the news that an acquaintance has placed a story in *Harper's* while we remain unpublished. Every writer skims interviews of new novelists to discern the author's age, and most suffer a blow if the New Star is younger than he or she. It is inevitable. Envy is, as Anne Lamott says in her revealing and witty book *Bird by Bird,* one of the occupational hazards of being a writer.

When others acquire what we desire, we are likely to stomp our feet, at least figuratively, and think, "It's unjust! I work harder/write better/am wiser/deserve it more than they! Look at me! *Me!* Not that jackass!" We rail at the debilitating forces in our past, irate with them for handicapping our competitiveness. We sometimes wish others ill, wickedly hoping their skill fades, or *Harper's* changes its mind, or the young New Star's next book is a highly publicized pile of dung.

If we are people of conscience, we experience these feelings, then hate ourselves for, as Anne Lamott puts it, oozing unhappiness like a sump. We shouldn't have this envy, we think; it is a crude, vulgar emotion that *other* people have. How could we—generous, friendly, politic we—possess the frozen smile and stilted "Con-grat-u-la-tions" of some slimy egotist? It jars our self-image. We gnash our teeth on the outside and grieve over our dead illusions about ourselves on the inside.

My student Marianne was so unable to endure her envy that she learned to make it her ally. After a friend of hers brought a story to class that was breathtakingly imaginative and well written, Marianne found herself fuming with envy. She drove home sweating, speechless, almost blind. Her friend had talent! Her friend had the admiration of the class! Marianne ran to bed, too full of fury and self-hate to speak to her husband. But after a night of inner screaming, she woke up into epiphany: She felt envy because she wanted—more badly than she had realized—to be a good writer. The extreme heat of her envy made her see just how much she wanted to succeed. So Marianne set herself to combatting envy with harder work and, instead of seeing her friend as someone to revile, saw her friend as a pioneer leading the way. And so Marianne turned the object of her envy into an object of inspiration.

As Bonnie Friedman says in her wonderful essay "Envy, the Writer's Disease," the remedy for envy is focusing on your own work. "Not the thinking about it. Not the assessing of it. But the *doing* of it. The answers you want can come only from the work itself. It drives the spooks away."

Left unaddressed, envy makes us feel alone and creatively clogged. We will become old before our time. We will intensify our impatience, thwart our contemplativeness, stunt all growth of confidence. We will forget that writing is something we do for *us*. We will see nothing beyond our own war with the world.

Euphoria: A gush of well-being and intense pleasure. Euphoria is writing afterglow, an unfurling of tranquility and happiness that follows the jangly tumult of writing, a time of radiance when all we want to do is breathe quietly and untangle ourselves from our pens and stare lovingly into the eyes of the world.

Euphoria comes when we have given our writing all we've got, and then still more. It comes after we have voyaged to themes we've never seen before and clambered through language combinations we've never heard before and unearthed bejeweled shadows of ourselves that were so buried we were startled to find they existed—and then we walk back into real life. So awestruck are we at the magic of writing, and so pleased are we by our own writing powers, that we feel dizzy with contentment, at peace with ourselves, and charmed by life in general.

Unlike contemplativeness or nimble-mindedness, euphoria can purr through us at any point in the writing process, from a moment after we finish a single session to a year after we have written a book. Euphoria can also last forever, or be as fleeting as a heartbeat. But brief or not, it makes the nonwriting part of life so sweet that we continue to strive for euphoria. Euphoria is what authors mean when they say they need writing to live. It is what rides them through the other hard emotions and makes the writing life a sane and uplifting choice.

Feelings of Failure: A shudder of vast disappointment in ourselves. We expect ourselves to be successful in our endeavors, yet we come to believe that we are not and will never be successful in writing. We thought we would be published by now, and since we're not, we must be washouts. Or we thought we would be able to write a competent story by now, but since we haven't, we must lack talent. Feelings of failure can pelt us at any moment for any reason and linger for any length of time. They make us sulk and despair and want to conceal our demoted-to-wretched self-image from others.

Every writer, no matter what level, struggles with occasional feelings of failure. Award-winning authors may panic that their newest story will be their last; beginning writers may drop a writing class after their first harsh critique. I myself felt like a failure the day I received my first rejections: a triple-whammy of no's from *Harper's*, *The Atlantic*, and *The New Yorker*. I also felt like a failure the day I completed the draft of a new novel and stumbled out of the library, moaning to myself the refrain from the twenty-something anthem by the solo artist Beck, "I'm a loser, baby, so why don't you kill me."

Feelings of failure are not logical. They are based on the assumption that now is the only time that counts—or that, if there *is* a future, it will feel no better than the present. I believed when I received the three rejection slips in one day that I had ample proof that I was a dud. I believed when I finished the draft of the novel that I had so much rewriting before me, I would never pull it off.

Beginning writers think that only they feel like failures. If they could get something published, they think, they would have validation and, hence, no more feelings of failure. Experienced writers know that feelings of failure are cyclical, and wait them out. Sometimes these feelings concern the marketplace, sometimes technical abilities, sometimes nothing we can determine. Feelings of failure waylay us like highway robbers. Eventually, though, we must duke it out with them so we can get back onto the road. (See "Tenacity" in chapter three.)

A former teacher gave me invaluable advice about feelings of failure. "Of course you have them," he told me when I returned to college for my ten-year reunion. "If you didn't have them from time to time, you wouldn't know you were trying. But the harder you try to succeed, the more often—and more spectacularly—you'll fail. All creative people cope with this. And if you don't find ways to work through those feelings and keep going, you *will* fail. Because you'll feel this way again and again, so you might as well learn to handle it now."

Or, as a student of mine once said, "The only difference between the successful and the failed is that when the successful fall down, they get back up."

Feelings of Inferiority: A shrinking of our self-esteem. We think others are better. Smarter, wiser, faster, more likable, more inventive, more talented, or just more. In our minds, we place ourselves beside them and they tower over us. In fact, we are barely visible. We slump, thinking of this. In the presence of those who are better than us, we may cower. We think there is so much we don't know and can't do. We think we are innately limited. We think we should melt away into gray and let the capable take over the earth.

When we feel inferior, we often feel anger at the same time. This might be directed at ourselves: *You moron! Why didn't you work on that paragraph longer? Or, What made you think you were NEA material? Any peabrain could see you're too dumb. And you're going to stay that way until you stop reading Spiderman and start reading Tolstoy, you jerk.* Sometimes, we direct the anger at those we deem superior: *He's just good because he's rich and doesn't have to work in some crummy office job like I do.* We feel anger toward editors who picked someone's work over ours and toward the world in general for giving us such a bum deal in life that we will never overcome our childhood.

Sometimes we try to compensate. We boast about every success, not to win support but to see other people's faces grimace with their own feelings of inferiority. We overeat or drink. We show people the same successful story over and over, trying to prove that once, in some shining, magical parting of our flaws, we could indeed match up.

Feelings of inferiority are delusion. They are based on the belief that each human being is one flat character, easily summed up. If there is one thing we can't do like a maestro, and do *right now*, then every aspect of us must be less than it should be. We find it impossible to believe that we could improve, or be only average in one area of our lives while still being highly competent in others. We find it so impossible, we settle into feeling inferior. Inferiority becomes our default emotion. It underlines our name. It becomes our home.

Frustration: Wanting, constipated. We feel frustration when we work and work and work on a piece and it just won't come together. We feel it when we submit our most praised story and it's rejected, maybe even summarily. Frustration is when something or someone keeps us from achieving our desired goal—the replacement of our trusted magazine editor with a new guy with new tastes, the lack of research material in the library, the limitations of our own skills. Frustration makes us feel annoyed and entrapped and powerless. It is anger locked in a cage.

We cannot fight frustration. We can forget about it during moments of celebration, and we can work our way out of it with patience (for both, see chapter three). But when we are in the heat of frustration, we cannot kick or bite or scream our way out of it. Like a Chinese finger box, the harder we fight it, the more stuck we feel. Sending indignant or defensive letters to editors who rejected us will not make their opinions of us become positive. Railing at the library director for the underfunded collection will not make reference librarians smile fondly upon us. And berating ourselves for our own limitations will only guarantee that we will stop trying.

Frustration comes when we partake too much of the *It was meant to be* school of philosophy and not enough of the *Oh, well, shit happens* one. If we acknowledge the latter, it's much easier to recognize that our path is being blocked and figure out an alternative path. If we're fixed on the former, we spiral from frustration into feelings of failure, and from there into complete inactivity of our pens.

Frustration can be a passing discouragement or a major downshift. It can be something we groan about with other writers or our impetus to bail out. It can last for a minute or forever. It can make us resentful and embittered and make all we love about life impossible to dredge out when we are writing.

Guilt: A parasitic gnawing of remorse. Guilt is chastisement we give ourselves; the most self-sufficient form of spanking ever devised by humankind. We feel guilt when our actions are in conflict with what we believe is the proper way for us to behave. Guilt tends to grip us subtly, vexing us long before we have identified it, and it lingers for ages, an uninvited guest with no intention of leaving.

In writing, guilt usually arises under two conditions. The first is when it contradicts other people's conceptions or expectations of us, and we have not yet fully given ourselves permission to go ahead anyway. Maybe our spouses think we should be spending our free time cleaning the house or earning money at a second job, but we would rather write. So we write, but with guilt. Maybe our family has always been secretive about cousin Julie's jail term and uncle Lenny's drinking. Yet we find such topics stimulating our ideas for a story, so we write the story, with guilt. Or we have trouble managing all our parenting tasks while still making the time to write. So we never have additional children to give our first child a sibling. We may then get our writing done, but do so with parental guilt.

Fortunately, guilt isn't a virus and, except for making us sigh over all that our family—or we ourselves—know we aren't doing, guilt cannot harm us creatively. Guilt is the hands of *No, you shouldn't!* closing around, but not choking, our imaginations. What hurts is not the actuality but the thought that maybe our imaginations *should* be smothered. Guilt cannot stop us; it just makes us think we ought to stop. But if we try to make use of it, guilt can trigger self-examination, leading us to understand why we aren't giving ourselves more permission, which in turn can cause us to decide what our priorities really are.

The other condition in which guilt occurs with writing is when we are *not* writing. We tell ourselves that we must finish the report for the boss instead, or take our friend out to dinner, or regrout the bathtub, so we don't ever get to the desk. We would if we had the time, of course, but alas, we cannot find the spare hour. We profess this, even though we suspect that we really *do* have the time but are making excuses and procrastinating. (Indeed, this form of guilt rarely occurs when we *truly* don't have the time.) We do not understand why we are making excuses; we guess we are procrastinating from feelings of inferiority or loneliness, but we can't or don't want to face the true reasons. So we don't write. Guilt floods in, and because we feel so guilty, we go to the movies or walk the dog—anything other than face the guilt, which means facing the page and *writing.*

As with the other kind of guilt, this affliction cannot hurt us. Sure, it might lead us to personify our computer, imagining that it whispers "Pssst!" to us every time we pass our desks, but guilt cannot delete our writing abilities, or sentence us to fire and brimstone, or trumpet to the world that we are not-writers. Guilt, in this case, is only a secondary emotion. It notifies us that we're not facing the real causes for our lethargy. If we let guilt become the main issue rather than merely the symptom, it will obstruct our understanding of why we procrastinate. If, however, we see it as the proverbial canary in the coal mine, we can get to work on excavating the root reasons behind our inaction. Only then can we take the final plunge away from guilt and into full commitment.

Insecurity: Conspicuous vulnerability. We don't hide insecurity, much as we want to. It trembles our smiles, ups our blowhard quotient, tilts our faces toward the dirt, wrests our pen away from the go-for-the-gold climax and handcuffs it to some soggy blah of an ending. When we feel insecurity, we hope we are straddling the fence between "I'm okay" and "I stink," but we know we are deep into "I stink." We are not unsure of ourselves; we are sure—sure that we are no good.

Insecurity is anticonfidence. In the alternate universe of insecurity, every comment and response to us triggers a wince, a further breaking down; it is confirmation of our worthlessness. We have heard the phrases "I'll show them" and "I think I can I think I can," but we know they don't apply to us. Even praise from a teacher or acceptance by an editor might inflame our insecurity: We think, *Oh, no! What if I can't do that again?* Many are the authors who ceased writing entirely after the first book was published. Insecurity engulfs us. We live in the belly of it and probably have for most of our lives. Hence, it seems impossible to smoke our way out, and instead we just let it grow larger.

Insecurity never exists without substantial conditioning, which, initially, we ourselves rarely provide. Our coaches were others we trusted. Parents or spouses or friends who reminded us that we were dense, a screwup, not nearly as smart as our older brother, a mistake they regret, going to send them to their grave for all the misery we've caused. Maybe they even found comic relief in our failures. (An award-winning novelist has an early memory that surges up at her deepest moments of insecurity: She is eight, lying in bed one night sobbing, while her mother and sister sit in the next room, laughing at a paper she had written for school, reading aloud the lines they are ridiculing.) Nothing we did elicited their good wishes or a hug.

So we tried to figure out how to win them over. We were exceptionally well behaved or exceedingly delinquent. We followed their rules meticulously, or we didn't listen to a word they said. Eventually, though, we taught ourselves that their approval would materialize after we became their accomplice in putting ourselves down. And so we came to believe we were indeed the oaf, the jerk, the crybaby, the nobody, the bossy bitch, the slug, the slut, the self-centered brat they thought we were. Maybe we even acted out those roles, or we acted out their opposites, trying to prove ourselves wrong. But the longer we go on without recognizing we've absorbed these negative self-images, the more deeply we believe we stink.

Unlike feelings of inferiority, insecurity in its purest form is seldom accompanied by anger. But anger toward those who pumped such self-doubt into us is one way we can recognize that we are trying to kill our insecurity: When, instead of nodding compliantly as Dad thunders about the B on our report card or our wife guffaws at our recounting of a compliment at work, we find ourselves glaring back, recognizing the cruelty and illogic of our loved one's response, *then* we know we are beginning to kick our insecurity habit.

Insecurity takes years to shake, and we can never be sure we won't fall under its power again. But we can try, especially by cultivating our inner voice, which is discussed in detail in the next chapter.

The more we question rather than acquiesce to our insecurity, the better our chance of succeeding.

Inquisitiveness: A continuous percolation of curiosity. We feel inquisitive when our writing gallops us into huge stretches of our own ignorance and we realize that the only way to press on is to fortify ourselves with knowledge. So we become more alert, read more widely, ask more questions. Each person on a bus, every conversation, all the billboards and bubble gum wrappers and skateboards glimpsed out of the corners of our eyes become source material. We want to know more. The superficial is not enough. We want to nose around into everything.

Inquisitiveness is one of most conspicuous and attractive advantages of writing. This is not because others see that our minds are hungry (after all, many people could care less about hungry minds). It is because when we are indulging in our inquisitiveness with others, asking them to explain how they learned to read fortunes from gypsies in Sarajevo, or to relate what happened during their nursery school graduation dinner, or to describe their first conversation with their grown sister after a six-year cold war, they see we are interested in them. "Oh," their eyes say, regaining some light they normally shutter out, "you want to know about *me?*" They are flattered.

Inquisitiveness, any social scientist can tell us, is at the heart of successful mingling. Everyone gains: our subjects, because they are honored by our interest, and we, too, because we are exploring uncharted parts of life, and because inquisitiveness helps make us new friends.

But inquisitiveness can, like witches, be either good or bad. Good inquisitiveness recognizes the subject's need for privacy and so steps ahead carefully, never aggressively, always with consideration. Bad inquisitiveness charges forward, even after discomfort has clearly arisen on the subject's face.

The only time bad inquisitiveness is allowable in writing is during investigative reporting, when, for instance, the mayor's evasiveness is obviously a cover-up for gross mismanagement. But bad inquisitiveness is not allowable—or flattering—during tea with Aunt Betsy, or after the man on the bus has said, "I don't want to talk about that." If we persist, we may still acquire information, but we will harden ourselves to the feelings of others, and so some humanity will leak away from our writing and our hearts, without our even noticing it.

At its best, inquisitiveness is a reaching forward with glee. It is an opening up, an enthusiasm for being students of life. The more inquisitive we are, the more stimulated we let ourselves be. It is a gift we give ourselves as well as others.

Laziness: A whine of inactivity. Laziness is not just idleness; it is always accompanied by the inner gripe of *But I don't want to.* While still children, we learned to associate laziness with tediousness: mopping the kitchen floor, writing thank-you notes for presents we never retrieved after they rolled under the sofa. So when we feel lazy with our writing, we tell ourselves we simply have a natural recoiling from tasks that are dull, which means that we are viewing writing as dull. All that slogging through the alphabet over and over, lashing our spritely imaginations to the heavy-jowled conventions of plot and character, suspending that interminable transition of a middle between the two shining towers of our beginning and our ending—and oh, don't even *talk* to us about revision! Writing is just inherently boring. Ask anyone. That's why we *don't want to* do it.

When we give in to laziness, we seldom ask ourselves the most fundamental question: If it's so boring, why do we want to do it? Instead, we seek reasons to explain our laziness. We are too busy shopping for new sneakers to have time to switch that story into third person. Or we need to help our friend out during the holiday rush in her store. Or we simply don't believe in plot. In other words, laziness is not *us*; it is the external forces of other obligations or the constraints of literary expectations. It is nothing we can do anything about, so we respond by doing nothing.

Some writers feel lazy during first drafts, and almost all writers feel lazy during revision. We set a kind of alarm clock in ourselves, and when we can't come up with a new word or narrative development fast enough—within a minute or month or whatever time limit we tacitly established for ourselves—we want to move on, regardless of whether we have taken the piece to its next level of quality. Often we even know what to do, yet we don't want to spend the time doing it. An urgency to complete cries out in us; we skate the surface to the end of the piece, rather than diving in for as long as it takes.

Laziness occurs when absurd expectations are courted by fear. We *should* be done with this story by now; since we can't puzzle it out, and we've been working at it *three whole weeks!* we conclude not that we need to learn patience, but that we must not be legitimate writers. Or: We *should* be able to write the story of our summer camp experience; after all, we've described the bug juice and raccoon raids and group showers to people a thousand times. But our terror at not being able to make our writing match our ambition is so great that instead of hunkering down and living out our writing commitment, we drop our pens, feeling listless, fatigued, unwilling.

In fact, I am not convinced that laziness per se really exists. I see it as yet another form of fear. We are so caught up in "shoulds" and so fearful that we can't achieve them that we just don't try.

My stepmother once described this mindset to me. When she was in college, she put off starting papers until the night before they were due. Then, of course, she had to grind until daybreak, inevitably producing work beneath her capabilities. But that was the point, she explained: Pressuring herself with the clock enabled her to avoid testing herself. She could always tell herself, "I *could* have gotten an A if I'd had more time." She would never know what she could truly do and could maintain her self-image without subjecting it to any challenges.

In writing fiction, we don't have a professor's deadline. Yet we tell ourselves we must finish by a certain (if ill-defined) time. This is so we never really see what we can do. It is so we can maintain our current construct of self. We justify, we blame, but really, we are simply too scared to find out that we might be less than we believe—even if it is at the expense of finding out that we might, in fact, be more.

Loneliness: A surge of desolation. Loneliness descends when we are sitting at the desk and we are seized by emptiness. *Nobody loves me,* we think. Or we worry, *If a writer writes in a room and no one hears him, maybe he doesn't exist.* We clench up; our pen seems to recede from us, leaving us focusing on the clumsy glove of our hand, or if we're on a computer, we cease reading the words on the screen and see only our reflection.

We tell ourselves this is because we are alone. We need officemates with whom we can shoot the breeze, an elevator operator who wants to hear about our date last night. We pick up the phone; we dwell on the film festival next week; we long for a more supportive spouse or, if we're single, any kind of spouse at all. Homo sapiens is a social animal, right? And we have it so hard. Other people who do their work around others, and who have a devoted someone to be with at night—they don't know what it's like. We know. Loneliness, we tell ourselves, is the price we pay for pursuing our literary dream.

Loneliness, however, only masquerades as the desire for company. It actually has little to do with whether or not others are accessible. Loneliness comes because we are inaccessible to ourselves. The word is a misnomer, since the root *lone* makes us think it is about being alone. But loneliness is not about being alone. As therapists like to point out, we can be in the middle of Grand Central Station and feel lonely, and we can be in a shack at the South Pole and not feel lonely. This is because loneliness is not about whether or not we are existing in a social context. Loneliness is about how we feel in the company of our selves. And if our selves feel empty, we interpret that emptiness as loneliness.

The reason we mistakenly associate loneliness with the lack of social interaction is because we imagine that the company of others will cure this emptiness. After all, we learned in the past that hanging out with loved ones helped us cope with misfortune. Emptiness, we think, must be treatable in the same way. We believe this even though we suspect that our loneliness is derived from a dislike of ourselves; that we are seeking distraction, not companionship. But admitting that would force us to reveal to ourselves that we are flawed. Thus we go on, yearning for others, wanting to escape the shell that we call our selves.

So intent are we on the elixir of social life that we neglect the best cure for loneliness: keeping company with our characters. Our characters are fragments of ourselves, grown large and complicated. When we are with them, we can't be lonely. They dance at a firemen's ball to which we are, at all moments, invited—and every one of them wants to dance with us. But if all we see are the flesh-and-blood people around us, we'll never get to the ball. In fact, the dance hall will remain empty, boarded up; we'll rush right by, not even noticing it is there.

Love/Hate: Contradictory epiphanies about our work. Love/hate can occur at any point in the writing process, from the first glimmer of an idea to the scrawling out of a draft to the final read-through of a piece that took ten years to complete. We become inflamed with the ingeniousness, coherence, seductiveness of the work until—maybe a second later, maybe a month—we become equally inflamed with its banality, sloppiness, inhospitality. *It's genius!* vies with *It's a bomb!* We berate ourselves for overjudging, and then, when we pendulum to the other side, for underjudging. Since we think we cannot be in two places at once, we question our perceptions, thinking, *now I see it clearly*, until now passes and we realize that we were wrong then, too.

Love/hate implies binary thinking. It is the same kind of thinking we have when we ask, "How are you?" We want others to say "Fine" or "Not so good" and are discomfited if they give both answers simultaneously or qualify that "fine" applies to certain aspects of their lives, "not so good" to others. We don't like that. We are not a manic sea, changing tides and spewing shells, furious at the shore and calm near the horizon. Our self-concept does not admit duality. No, we are a neat little swimming pool: contained, placid, the same forever.

A few years ago I rebelled against the usual responses to "How are you," which, I felt, forced me to deny the possibility of change. Instead, I began viewing my response in terms of a continuum, ranging from "It sucks" to "It rocks." I told people this is how I would answer "How are you?" from now on, with the qualifier that my answer would count only as an emotional snapshot of this one moment in time; after now, they should expect my position on the continuum to change.

Love/hate is not, as we believe, a repeating pattern of seeing more clearly, reversing our previous opinions, and then seeing the opposite. Love/hate is the hermaphrodite of opinion. We can love many aspects of a piece of writing while we hate others. We can also love and hate the same aspects simultaneously.

The grander our aspirations and the longer we work on a piece, the more frequently and intensively we will experience love/hate. It then feeds itself, because the more we feel love/hate, the more we want to write: If we hate how we handled emotion, or dialogue, or whatever, in this one piece, maybe we can try to do better tomorrow or with the next piece, always aiming to tilt the balance toward love. Love/hate, then, can be well utilized if combined with a strong commitment to writing. In addition, our ability to tolerate love/hate can teach us that we are indeed able to function, and function beautifully, when we accept the existence of our inner contradictions (a useful bit of knowledge to have throughout our lives).

The only disadvantage to love/hate is when it comes before or during the first draft. Then, we are so pushed and pulled that we often drop the story entirely. Then love/hate abandons its roles of guide and commentator. It becomes censor and executioner. We have seen our ally and made it into our end. (For clues on surviving this problem, see "Hearing Your Inner Voice" and "Delusions of the Creative Process," both in chapter seven.)

Meaningfulness: A glow of dignity from engaging in purposeful activity. Meaningfulness can spring up suddenly while we are flying through the first draft of our story or rise slowly after we have polished an entire novel. It can come at any moment when we know we have done ourselves, and maybe the world, good, that we set out to perform a task that we hoped would give our lives a greater sense of importance and value, and that, having accomplished the task, we indeed feel important and valued.

Many beginning writers are drawn to writing because they feel that they live mundane lives of no significance, or what I, looking at myself, used to call a "small life." We think that no one but our friends will ever know or care that we lived. We look for ways to transcend our smallness. Perhaps we fancy being an inventor of culture-altering gadgets or the discoverer of new laws of physics. I used to wish I could run a three-minute mile, and sing with four voices at once, and found a new calendar. We want to go beyond the wheres and whatfors of our lives, maybe not so people know us, but so we can feel we have done something significant for humanity and ourselves. Or, as I used to wish when I was in a long writer's block, so we can feel we are doing what we were put here to do.

We think writing is an ideal route to provide this meaning, and we are not mistaken. As writers throughout history have attested—and as we ourselves can learn over our writing years—writing does transform readers' lives, in big ways and small. Books taught my family how to raise a puppy. Stories by Chekhov encouraged one friend to be a doctor. A biography by C.S. Lewis impelled another friend to become a Christian. George Orwell's *1984* galvanized me to turn off my television; *Grimm's Fairy Tales* prompted me to knead my imagination to life; Vladimir Nabokov's *Lolita* taught me to feel sympathy for the most odious of characters; Patrick Süskind's *Perfume* made me remember the neglected organ of my nose.

Meaningfulness can also arise from the very process of writing. In this case, it is *our* lives, not readers', that then experience meaning. Whether we are published or not, over time the act of sitting, pondering, eliminating our internal clock, following our instincts, and working hard can give us a sense of purpose. And this alone may be the meaning we seek.

Sometimes we forget about pursuing meaningfulness when we're writing. We may forget for twenty years. Then one morning, when we hit an exquisite metaphor, or one of our readers sends a letter swooning over our work, or someone tells us that our story made him take care of an emotional act that he had long put off doing, we feel as if some kind of sun has risen inside us: *Aha!* we think, grinning, *now I know why I do this!*

Meaningfulness cannot be planned for or pursued. But when it emerges, it stretches us tall, infuses us with confidence, makes us work harder. It connects us to all people with missions, from artists to scientists to revolutionaries. It makes every day count, life forever worth living. It inspires us as much as it rewards. It is our bar mitzvah into continuing.

Nimble-mindedness: Dancing fandangos in the mind. Nimble-mindedness means we are thinking swiftly and lightly, speeding over and through multiple thoughts like a pollinating Mercury, all the while maintaining the wit and spiritedness of Pan. When we are nimble-minded, every word, idea, character trait, narrative development—everything—becomes our mental playground to leap and slide through, to crawl and limbo under, to twist and juggle around.

The world feels fully elastic to us; nothing seems formidable, let alone frightful, because everything is malleable, and everything is play.

Nimble-mindedness first sprouts in us soon after we have begun writing for the first time and see that writing entails knocking down all the *Do Not Trespass* signs and skipping, tentatively and then wildly, everywhere we have been afraid to go before. We realize we can vandalize every social convention, hot-wire sleeping thoughts, challenge language to a chicken race, let all our most secret voices dare to roar. Soon our minds get a taste for this mischievousness. We like it so much, we want more of it. And so the longer we write over the years, and the more wayward our minds become, the more we invent our own understanding of language and story, and the more nimble our minds grow.

Nimble-minded people make rapid connections between seemingly disparate elements. They think original thoughts. They admit what they do not know because they are confident that they can learn. They are not afraid.

Paranoia: A chronic tic of looking over one's shoulder. Paranoia tells us that the worst-case scenario will always happen, so we'd better watch out—even though our vigilance won't prevent the disaster, nor will it lighten the damage. The magazine will lift an idea from our spaceship-in-the-Grand-Canyon story and win a major award for their staff's rewrite of our material; the family will stop speaking to us and omit us from all future Sunday barbecues; the FBI will root out one of its Ten Most Wanted from our acknowledgments and lock him up for twenty years; the friends will see themselves behaving unbecomingly in our infidelity-on-the-beach scene and sue us into homelessness. We will offend or provoke. We will be on our way, and then *they* will make us fail.

Paranoia is no more about the machinations of nefarious others than loneliness is about the absence of social stimulation. Paranoia is about our fear of giving writing our all. We use paranoia as a handy mental device when we have been striving and sweating and drawing together and just as we begin actually getting somewhere, we stop. We tell ourselves that if we finish this story, we will fall prey to lawsuits or ostracism, but in truth, we are simply afraid of going on.

This is not to say that the chop-shop boss won't send out thugs if he reads the story based on our spying at his garage, or that our next-door neighbor won't burst out sobbing when she comes across her husband's put-downs in our dialogue. But paranoia is what we feel when we dread the worst before it shows any hint of occurring and then curtail our ambitions so we never have to encounter what isn't yet there.

Paranoia is a form of fear that is based on a grandiose sense of our own importance. We think that when we publish a story, the world will notice. Indeed, the world will notice so dramatically that *they will come after us*, or, indeed, that they will plagiarize us. We will attend a movie two years hence and see our story, the same one we couldn't sell to anyone, on the screen! A world-famous author will come across our book proposal, write the book we wanted to write, and make ten million dollars! This is far more conceivable to us than the possibility that no one will notice our work at all.

We forget that other people are so caught up in their own lives, they seldom care what we are doing. We forget that, as passionately as some people read, very few carry that passion into action, especially action against the author. And very few would need or want to filch our ideas. Hollywood, and big-name authors, and anyone else whose plagiarism of our work would lead to great financial loss for us— these people have no scarcity of ideas. They don't need us. We forget that the big battle is just to get people to recognize our work exists, not to cringe from the ramifications of their recognition.

Or, as I tell myself whenever paranoia seeps into my thoughts, "Someone cares that much about your work and thinks others will care, too? Thumbs up, Simon. You should always be so lucky."

Passion: Enthusiastic and enduring literary libido. We love writing so much, we want to do it whenever we can. At the desk, on the train, in the bath, while walking. We feel best when writing; it soothes and expands us, connects us to the world and ourselves, makes us thrill to mess and humanness, nudges us into commitment. We see it as a lover, giving and forgiving, cerebral and sensuous, its face always before our eyes, its embrace the one we want most. If we have actual lovers or spouses, sometimes we feel we're cheating on them, given our passion for our linguistic paramour. Our real-life lovers might even feel threatened; possessive ones may interrupt our writing to ask us to join them on the porch for a pitcher of lemonade or to make love. They may want us to limit our rendezvous time; they may boycott all mention of their rival. They may even, if they are deeply insecure, read our creations only to mock them.

Other people do not understand our passion, especially if we are beginning writers. They see it as a transient fancy, like our five childhood classes in the clarinet or our interest in Thai cooking a year ago. They are amused and often supportive, yet might try to lure us away from our desk. "We're having brunch, and it won't be complete without *you*." "You mean you won't be available for *weeks*? But I'm dying to tell you about my daughter's honeymoon!" They call on the phone and launch instantly into conversation, neglecting to ask if we're free. They act like the drinking mates of alcoholics who are trying to go sober: "Come on, one little drink won't hurt you."

The difference is that alcoholism is a behavioral disorder. Writing is a behavioral *order*. Social temptations won't wrest it completely out of our lives, but if indulged in often and without thought, they will make us see writing as a ball and chain rather than wings. Passion is one of the only ways to resist temptation.

Every concern that a writer has about writing ultimately comes down to passion. *How do I find the time?* and *How can I do it when my family doesn't support me?* and *How could lowly, little me feel important enough to write?*—all those questions are intimately connected to *If you really want to write, you'll find a way.* The same applies to technical matters. Don't know how to handle suspense? Sentence variety? Shifting time periods? *If you really want to write, you'll find a way.* You'll be resourceful. You'll put yourself in a mental school where all the pupils are yourself, toss out all the lesson plans that have been passed on to you, and dream up an innovative curriculum of your own. And if that doesn't work, you'll try and try until you hit on something that does.

Although we often feel heady eruptions of passion while writing any one story, we know we are passionate about writing when our desire to write refuses to die over many years. It may fade—when we first begin absorbing the shock of rejection slips, simply can't make a story come together, are newly involved with a sweetheart or job or infant—but if it is truly passion, it will never go away. A year after the rejection slips, when we're washing our hands in the restroom at work: *Yes! I've got to get back!* The newborn child takes a nap, and we snatch up the pen instead of a broom. Two decades after a teacher brandished our story during a lecture on bad metaphors, we still want to write.

Passion is both the chicken and the egg. We must have passion if we persist, and we must persist if we have passion. It ebbs and flows, like passion in a marriage. But if it is true passion, it remains with us until death do us part, our appreciation for it only deepening as we age.

Pride: Ego in a contest with others. Whereas ego is about our own sense of perfection, pride is about our sense that others are not as perfect as we. We gaze down on them from above, eagle-eyed, searching their work for the desiccated, the unweeded, the fallow, the overtilled. If we pick out flaws, we are pleased, because then we know once again that we are king of the mountain. If we *don't* pick out flaws, we tell ourselves that all we need is more information about this other writer—her sexual history, his relationship with his mother—so that we can tell ourselves, *Yeah, he may be a good writer, but he's not a nice person,* and give ourselves one more reason to dismiss anyone who is not us.

Pride is faith in our superiority. We are not slipshod or slothful, the way others are. We get our stories right. We know how to do it. What a pity for others that they don't have our intelligence and experience. Everything they tell us is a pockmarked reflection of something we have done better, or worked at harder, or suffered with longer. No one is in our league. We let others know that, perhaps subtly; even when we're responding to their concerns, we begin most of our sentences with "I."

Of course, when we crown ourselves and use our vaulted position to judge others, we also sentence ourselves to perfection. We must be right, and if we're not, well . . . we *must* be right. Consequently, we dam off the possibility of learning. No teacher, or fellow writer, or even quiet doubt in our own heads can tell us we need to make changes in a piece or work harder. This is how we do it, period. If we ask to hear opinions, it is because we're hoping to be applauded, even celebrated, for our flawlessness. Should the opinions lean toward *More work, please,* we snarl and walk away. *Other* people may need more work. *Other* people make mistakes. Not us. We are fully formed. And anyone who can't see that is as flawed as those whose work is less than our own.

Pride kills writers. It chains them onto a single plateau of development and keeps them there till they waste away into bones. They could escape before that fate, but pride insists that this one plateau is all. They need only take a swig of humility and imperfection to loosen those chains and climb to the next plateau, but to do that they must admit they are no better than others, and pride tells them that they mustn't.

Pride is actually its own opposite. Instead of being about superiority, it is about inferiority: We are so concerned that we don't match up that, in fact, all we do is match ourselves. We also imagine that others are doing the same, and because we must come out as Number One, we separate ourselves from the rest of humanity, wedging us off from the universality of emotions and experience, corralling ourselves into the narcissistic.

When I meet with students for the first time, I ask them to admit to their own imperfection. "I'm imperfect," I tell them, "and I expect no more of you." But we all begin writing with a great deal of pride, and it takes a long time and a lot of effort before we can fully erode it.

Shame: Panic arising from others' realizing that we are a fraud. Shame ambushes us when we are unable to sell the story everyone loved, or we write a violent confrontation that the teacher tells the class is "beneath you," or we publish a book that goes out of print within a year. We recognize that people who previously saw us as exceptional might defrock us to the merely mediocre. And we are afraid this will lead to their liking us less—or perhaps not at all.

Shame necessitates myth. We have created a myth of ourselves (or not dissuaded others from creating a myth of us) as capable, a golden girl or boy, a natural writer, a success in the making. We believe that other people need myths so they can keep going themselves: Mythical stories of triumph and fame make them feel that the world is not such a bad place after all, that there *is* justice and perhaps a grand plan, that good things happen to those who deserve it, that maybe they can become something themselves. We allow ourselves to be other people's models, the fuel they need to persevere or, at least, to maintain optimism. And so we cringe and grow nauseated at the thought of others' seeing our failures; we know that if their myth of us goes into a nosedive, their disappointment will be vast, having implications far beyond their opinion of us.

Or so we tell ourselves. In reality, we feel shame because we want to be liked. We use our writing talents and successes to draw people to us, to be our morale boosters, our friends; if, we fear, we are perceived as a failure, we will lose all those smiling faces and be left with nothing but our own frown.

Shame roots itself in our tendency to seek ourselves in the eyes of others. If they like us, we like us. If they walk away from us, we must be unlikable. So we guard the way others see us because we need to guard the way *we* see us. And since we want to see ourselves as perfect, we want others to know only that which will ensure that they see us as perfect too.

Some years ago when I was in a crisis, a friend gave me the single most helpful piece of advice I could tell myself. She was in a Twelve Step program, which I credit with giving her this clarity. "What other people think about you," she said, "is none of your business." And she was right: My return to emotional stability depended on my remembering the boundary between my self-image and others' thoughts (real or imagined) about me. (See "Boundaries," chapter three.) To focus on what others think of us is to deemphasize, forget, or negate what *we* think of us. Their opinions of us are unimportant. Only *our* opinions of us are important. We may sometimes disappoint ourselves, but if we do so without shame, we can learn from our mistakes that much more effectively.

Spiritual Connectedness: An apprehension of human or cosmic Oneness. This can take the form of an anthropological revelation, e.g., pain is pain and joy is joy, no matter our age or ethnic group or gender or background; or it can take a more mystical, almost religious, form, i.e., all experience and time and matter is interrelated, expressions of the same larger, perhaps godlike, phenomenon. Spiritual connectedness can occur in a single, blinding moment, a *Tah-dah!* when some heretofore unconceived unity becomes quite apparent. It can also rise up slowly, subtly, an *Oh, I get it now* that can persist for years.

However it arrives, spiritual connectedness tends to wait until the writer has been writing a long, long time. Beginning writers almost never feel it; they look at experienced writers who seem to have a sense of tranquility and understanding, and they shudder, believing that their own low self-esteem will prevent them from ever feeling this. They don't realize it is a state of being that writers work up to and that no one plans for or thinks about until it happens.

Spiritual connectedness is perhaps the most monumental reward of writing. As John Gardner comments in *On Becoming a Novelist,* writing is less a profession than a yoga, or "way," a quasi-religious "alternative to ordinary life-in-the-world." Writing is an activity, he asserts, with "spiritual profits."

Spiritual connectedness grows out of the setting aside of pride and ego; the admitting of imperfection; the nurturing of contemplativeness, euphoria, inquisitiveness, and meaningfulness; and the deeply felt acknowledgment that we are all just as fearful and hopeful and struggling and loving as everyone else. Spiritual connectedness leads to an extreme comfort with the world that transcends writing and publishing. It does not make us cozy up to everyone—we know, since we have seen our own shadow so closely, that everyone has a dark side, and that some dark sides should be circumvented to avoid inviting our own injury. But it makes us look into the faces of others and see ourselves, and look into our own face and see others. It enables us to write from many points of view and demographic profiles, to walk up to strangers and quickly find something we have in common, to live without the anxiety of being found a fraud, to experiment in our work without an aching for acceptance. We accept ourselves as we accept others, and when others don't accept us, we no longer doubt ourselves as a result.

I felt the anthropological form of spiritual connectedness when I was writing my first book, but not until I was hammering out the revision of my second book did I feel a cosmic form as well. I am not a religious person; most of my life I have questioned, or maybe even scoffed at, the concept of God. Yet the more deeply I wrote, and the more I lowered myself through the layers of character and narrative and language, the more I felt I'd come into contact with something divine. It was as though my book already existed in some great cosmic library, and I was just groping my way through some haze to make a copy of it. For several months I felt as if I was in a writing trance so deep that I'd entered the world of dreams, and then, after some more months, that I was dreaming so fluidly that I had passed into the collective unconscious. There I was, swimming in some great All, unhampered by "I" or time, patient, free of fear, enjoying it.

The result was that I lost a lot of the angst that had depleted me for much of my life. All my anger toward other people subsided; I came to regard their failings as being on a par with my own, and so found myself feeling compassion for them, as I was no longer oppressed by their past errors. I was also able to let go of several relationships that had weighed me down; I saw I could like people without necessarily wanting to be friends with them. I lost my paranoia and shame, my reliance on external validation to accept myself. I acquired a tremendous comfort with my own solitude, and a sense of inner calm in all my social interactions. I learned I could change my mind and not hate myself; peek behind facts and see the contradictions lurking there. I could tolerate paradox, continually challenge who I am. Start embracing. Stop fretting.

In the year or two after I finished that book, people would often ask me how I became like this. After seminars and classes, or even overhearing me in a coffeeshop: "You have such a groundedness," they'd remark, "the peace of someone who's a lot older than you. How did you manage that? How did you get so wise?" I'd pause and mull it over; wisdom was not a trait I'd ever attributed to myself.

I'd cast about for a profound response but when I opened my mouth, I'd give the only answer that made any sense to me. "Writing," I'd say. "That about sums it up." And then if they wanted to know more, I'd try to explain what that meant.

CHAPTER THREE

THE GENERAL ANTIDOTES

W̲e now know the big emotions and states of mind that all writers experience and have seen that the difficult ones result from a dismal self-image and counterproductive behaviors.

This chapter elaborates on revising our self-image and behaviors so that they can help rather than hinder us. It consists of several self-contained entries, most of which refer to certain negative emotions discussed in chapter two. In addition, each entry implicitly addresses *all* the negative emotions. Whichever way you read them—as specific prescriptions for specific ailments or as general recommendations for any and all kinds of writer-related maladies—you should feel, after you look through this chapter, stronger and more directed on how to work through the more challenging emotions.

Boundaries: A psychological map in which each individual is a sovereign state with clearly defined borders, which no other individual can pillage, invade, conquer, or enslave without permission. When we have boundaries, we set limits on how other people may treat us, limits that have at their core the inviolable principle of self-respect. We respect ourselves so much that we do not do or feel what others pressure us to do or feel unless *we* want to. We do not give in to our classmates' demands that we wear penny loafers simply because they want us to be part of the crowd; when our spouses browbeat us into watching TV though we'd rather read the paper, we don't crumple up the paper and sigh, "Well, it doesn't matter to me anyway"; when our neighbors nominate us to chair the planning committee despite our well-known aversion to meetings, we don't say yes to be nice; if we announce to our parents that we're moving out and they respond, "If you move, you'll give me a heart attack!" we don't buckle. We don't let others' feelings and desires bleed into and overtake ours. We don't confuse our responsibilities with their manipulations. We don't "go along." We choose.

Of course, boundaries work both ways. When we have a clear sense of boundaries, we do not try to boss anyone else around. No more bullying our younger sister to get us the glass of water that we could get ourselves. No more glowering our co-workers into submission. No more pretending we haven't heard our friends say, "I don't want to" and just bulldozing ahead with what *we* want. We cease living in any way that demotes others to a position beneath us and instead give everyone just as much respect as we give ourselves. Boundaries are how we manifest, without coercion or cynicism, the wisdom of the Golden Rule.

In the writing life, boundaries are invaluable. When we first start writing, they enable us to make time: We set up moats across which none can trespass, regardless of how they fascinate, order, or beg us. We tell them we will be happy to clean our room, make dinner, go to a party, or listen to how their husband forgot their anniversary— but not now; we're going to write now. Boundaries let us say, "Sorry, but I must." Boundaries help us hang up the phone, close the door, sit off in the corner of the cafe. Boundaries give us the permission to make priorities.

After we have written for years, boundaries are useful in other ways. Our writing class implicitly tells us that stories should be written in *this* style; an editor informs us that novels are worthy only if they're on *these* kinds of subjects. We become intimidated by what we think might be other people's wisdom. We want to discard our own thoughts—*do it right.* Put on their literary penny loafers instead of the cowboy boots we prefer, even if we have to slice off our toes to do so. Then, they will like us. We will be one of them.

We are drawn to be subsumed because, for most of us, it is easier to figure out what another (or several others) wants and likes than to figure out what we ourselves want and like, easier to be part of a stream than to be a single, finding-its-own-way raindrop. It takes concentration and practice to learn our own wants and desires, and few of us are eager to put in the effort. Only when we see the ill effects of being absorbed by others do we see the point in understanding ourselves.

Boundaries give us a sense of solidness from which we can make decisions. We are not as susceptible to being talked into ill-advised behaviors; we persevere with our writing regardless of intrusions or bribes. I screen phone calls during my writing time so I don't accidentally get sucked into an hour-long conversation. Most writers do not talk about what they're writing until they are ready to do so. I rarely accept social invitations the minute they are offered, and instead get back to the host after I have assessed whether I can afford the time away from my work. Some writers work behind a closed door on which they hang a DO NOT DISTURB sign, or if that doesn't establish boundaries, they write in a location away from their house. Many highly productive authors maintain their level of output by, in part, listening politely to people's suggestions about what they should write next (and people are always making such suggestions, from editors to spouses to strangers on the swivel stool at the diner) and then writing what they want to write anyway.

Boundaries, once established, are the best way we have to discover and accomplish what we want. They allow us to arrest the damaging effects of competitiveness, envy, feelings of inferiority, guilt, paranoia, shame, and all other negative emotions triggered by our interactions with other people. Boundaries release us from the influence of others and place us in custody of ourselves. They are the draperies we close on the world so we can walk around in the nude. They are the sound-proof doors we lock so we have the freedom to sing. They are the room of our own, our clean and well-lighted place, the privacy to find ourselves in our own ink.

Celebration: Making a big deal out of every accomplishment. Success does not come around very often in writing. We may realize this after we've slaved for months to finish a story that still feels off, or after we've received rejections for all our stories. Whatever the stimulus, early in our careers we see that most of our writing time is spent on trying—and growing frustrated—and very little on savoring completion or fame. Celebration is how we acknowledge every single distinction. It is the way we exile those feelings of frustration, which helps us push through frustration when we reencounter it later, even if our respite lasted only a few hours or days.

When I teach at a university, I put celebration into the curriculum: On the dates when the major revisions are due (which everyone in the class must turn in, on predetermined dates, three times a semester), I cancel regular classwork and throw a party, with coffee and pastries and literary games. Triumph happens so rarely, I tell my students, that we must rejoice when it does—and revising a story by its deadline is a triumph, worthy of chocolate eclairs and parlor games.

Many moments qualify as writer triumphs. Some are obvious: acceptance of our stories by a magazine, notification of our selection by a grants organization, a contract from a film company. Some moments are not as blatant: An author we love, whose last novel prompted us to write a fan letter, sends a warmhearted reply; a reporter who once mentioned our name in a brief item on local writers recognizes us in a store, comes over, and wishes us well; we receive a rejection letter full of effusive handwritten compliments, a request to stay in touch, and a signature; we deliver an energetic reading. All are triumphs. All deserve not just recognition, but fanfare.

I usually commemorate the small to mid-sized successes with exultant calls to friends, and then I break out the sparkling cider. When it comes to the big bonanzas—selling a book or an option for a movie—I treat myself to a gift: a pair of glass earrings I had coveted for ages; a week's trip to England; a new computer. Whatever the rites are, I want them to stand out in my memory, to shout, *Remember that day? I'm a reminder that you can do it.*

That is celebration: a ritual of acknowledgment that it's not all dark, creepy forests with malevolent trees and flying monkeys; that sometimes, when we work really hard and hold onto our pluck and stay alert and are touched by the hand of good fortune, we can reach the Emerald City and indulge in magnificent revelry.

Commitment: A promise to ourselves that our writing matters profoundly and that, come what may, we will honor that promise. We know down to the lining of our soul that we are devoted to our writing, that we cleave unto it, that we need it, that we cannot wash it out of our hair, that it's an itching in our heart, that it says *yes* when everyone else says *no*, that it shows us light where others see dark, that it makes us think in complex harmony.

So we commit ourselves to it. Yes. I will. And we do not waver, even though the world sometimes seems to want us to.

Commitment isn't necessary in the easy times; when the kisses flow daily, who needs a wedding ring? Commitment is necessary only in times of trouble. Laziness is etherizing our will. Our love/hate is listing toward hate. Guilt is tugging us toward inoffensive dullness. Paranoia is shackling our productivity. Shame has us shivering from multiple rejection wounds. Or friends are tempting us away.

This is when we need commitment. Without it, we push back from the desk, shrug off the unfinished novel. Who cares. We don't. We were only dating writing anyway. Maybe she's not the girl for us. Besides, she requires too much effort. If we wanted to work so hard, we'd get a job laying bricks, not waste our time fooling with such an elusive and temperamental lover.

Of course, writing is both fooling with a lover *and* laying bricks. And if we are to avoid that struggle of getting started *again*, we need to commit to writing during the lover phase. When we're tingling from our attraction to writing, swooning with intoxication, ripping off our self-censors, forgetting our wanting-to-be-liked prophylactics, *that* is the time to commit. We want it. We want it so bad that we agree to want it as much in the future as we do now. We promise we will.

Having made ourselves this promise at a time of joy, we are better able to stick it out when we hit those stretches of monotony or angst. We remember how good it felt, and we know that if we keep going, we will have those feelings again.

But unlike discipline or a Las Vegas marriage, commitment doesn't happen in a flash. Only when we have revisited the delicious delirium of writing many times over do we realize that we must really want it for good. Writing, we see, gives us a cyclical return of romance. Say yes and we get not a settled marriage, but a string of honeymoons that goes on forever.

Discipline: The routine action by which we prove our commitment. Without discipline, no number of vows, wishes, or stories-yearning-to-be-written will amount to anything. We can talk all we want, sob about our unfulfilled ambition, sign a pledge that we will get to work. But it's all bluster and nonsense unless we *act*. And the most effective initial act is to establish discipline.

When people at parties hear that I'm a writer, they usually respond with, "I always wanted to write but I lack discipline." They speculate on why I have the ability to foil diversion. I must have an abnormal quantity of self-control, they suggest; been raised with a Puritan work ethic; nod off at the first sign of fun; be a stoic, a masochist. They can hardly believe it when I laugh.

People have the erroneous idea that discipline is a quality that we either possess or we lack, like symmetrical facial features or small feet. But discipline is an acquired trait. It is a logical carrying through of a decision; the implementation of a choice. Discipline results from realizing that, when we want something badly enough, the action required to get it is not a burden but a vehicle. And it is up to us to make that vehicle a creaky, leaky jalopy or a humming, vrooming cruisemobile.

Discipline is commitment to routine. We have routines for many things: brushing our teeth, riding the bus to work, watching certain TV shows. All it takes to "get" discipline is to plan a routine and decide to stick to it. Discipline is a single decision. It is not something we select over and over, each day facing a new mountain of hesitations and resistances and enticements. We decide at one important moment that we are going to act, and then every day we renew that decision by acting. That is discipline. If we decide to act and do *not*, it doesn't mean that we lack discipline; it means that we lack desire. (For suggestions on practical approaches to establishing discipline, see "Finding Time to Write" in chapter four.)

Humility: Acceptance that we are never the master but always the student. Humility is not merely the opposite of arrogance; humility is also the compatriot of confidence. Without humility, we sometimes begin a story bloated with ego and pride, thinking, "I've pulled this off before, I can do this better than anyone, this'll be rolling off a log," and then, when we wade deeper into the challenges of these particular characters or narrative developments, we fume. How could we be so stupid! So mistaken! So conceited! Only when we accept that writing is *always* a challenge, regardless of our previous successes, can we keep producing.

Humility is awe for the void of the blank page. Awe—not fear. Humble writers don't quake at the task of filling that page. They embrace it, and with reverence, knowing that it has slain many a literary dream. Humble writers admit that maybe they *don't* know. They see that the longer they write, the more they need to learn. That their ego matters less than each individual story. That the striving never ends. What ends are the excess of bravado that they can pull it off without effort and the lack of faith that they can't pull it off no matter what. What comes is humility, which they've learned is not just the path away from ego and pride, but is also the path toward faith.

I first met humility in college. I'd survived freshman year with great difficulty but I *had* survived, and somehow this achievement convinced me that all would be smooth sailing now. Thus, sophomore year, my attitude toward school became one big *No problem.* Maybe other people needed to spend seven hours in the library, but not I. I was more together than they. I had this down. So smug was I that I delayed starting my end-of-the-semester papers. Then finals week slammed into me, and only then, desperate and terrified, did I knuckle down and get to the library. Smugness, I saw, doesn't get papers written, ego doesn't construct paragraphs, pride doesn't compose coherence. Only hard work does. I later learned that this phenomenon has the misnomer "sophomore slump," a term that implies laziness. But it wasn't laziness that caused my sophomore slump; it was excessive assurance without labor. Finally, I admitted I needed to work, and since then, I have never suffered in that way again.

Humility keeps us moving forward. It strips away our lies and boasts. It comes with experience and gives a perspective that never quits. It keeps our eyes down on our pen, critical and focused, instead of gazing with adoration at our mirror.

The Inner Voice: The internal aesthetic trail guide that directs us toward the great. Beginning writers often question their ability to tell when a piece is done. They ask others, "Do you think it's ready?" They frequently back away from making their own artistic judgments as well, asking others, "Do you like it?" figuring, Others must know more than I. They know they need to develop what Hemingway called the "built-in shock-resistant shit detector" but aren't sure how. Insecurity ricochets inside them, sometimes occasionally, sometimes continuously. They cannot imagine how they will ever *know.* And all because they have not yet learned that every writer has an inner voice that does our shit detecting and delivers our declarations of completion. It leads each of us away from sounding like anyone else and ferries us to our unique vision.

One of my most successful stories was pshawed by the writing class I was in at the time. If I'd believed their opinions were more "correct" than mine, I would have tossed the story instead of working on it more and sending it off to a contest—a contest I won and that soon led to my first book contract. But I believed in the story because (although I didn't know the concept at the time) my inner voice told me it was good, original—in need of revising but essentially on its way.

I didn't develop the concept of the inner voice until I was crawling through the revision of my novel. Although I had been writing for twenty years, I still couldn't ascertain when I hit or missed. But during that revision, I decided to stop showing my work to other people until I was completely satisfied. Instead, I would read the piece *out loud* to an audience of me. This would, I guessed, force me to lean entirely on myself, both for figuring out what was wrong and for figuring out how to fix it.

So, in private, I read the novel aloud over and over and over, concentrating every time on how each word, sentence, paragraph, and section felt to me. After months of this, I realized that an inner voice was speaking back to me. Actually, it wasn't a voice as much as a little squeak. *Eeek,* it would sound when I reread a certain paragraph, *that doesn't feel quite right.* Or *Eeek, too much description.* At first, the squeak was subtle; I'd tell myself I wasn't hearing anything and continue. By the tenth time I reread the piece, the squeak would be a shout; by the hundredth, a military command. Finally I'd get so sick of hearing it that I'd fix the damn paragraph. Then I'd go back to rereading and wrestle with new squeaks. Again and again.

In time, I saw that I was cultivating my inner voice. The more I listened to it—the gulps that I hadn't pulled off that metaphor, the *tsk*s that the humor wasn't truly funny, the *No, that's not it*s when I tried certain narrative developments—and the more rapidly I reacted, layer after revising layer, the clearer the voice grew inside me. Eventually, this led not only to my knowing when the piece was done, but to finding and burrowing into a new vision, something unlike anything I'd read (or certainly written) before. Which led to my developing confidence.

I am forever watching people train themselves to gag their inner voices. They prepare a story for their writing class. Before they turn it in, I ask, "How do you feel about it?" They say, "Well, I'm not sure about the ending." I say, "Maybe you should keep working until you're sure." "Nah," they say, "I'm going to take it into class and see what *they* think." Which in practice means that, if class finds the ending good enough, the writer trains himself to disregard his inner voice. So he never pushes the piece to a new height, never finds a vision beyond the one the class already sees. The same problem arises if the class thinks the ending needs work and offers a specific solution; instead of working harder on her unique approach, the writer reorients the piece as the class wants, mulching the very traits she could otherwise let blossom into a singular vision.

Just because someone likes a line in our story doesn't mean we should keep it. And if we feel moved to give a writer ideas for revision, we should give two or three at least, so we never forget that solutions are infinite, limited only by the adventurousness of the writer's inner voice.

A beginning writer needs to be careful, however, not to mistake laziness for the inner voice. The latter comes through a great deal of hard work. If a class says a piece doesn't feel right, a writer will just thwart his own progress if he shrugs, "My inner voice told me to do it that way, and if you don't think it works, tough noogies." If others don't think a piece works, it's possible (and, if we haven't put in months of concentrated effort, quite likely) that it needs more work, more deliberation, *more attention paid to the inner voice.* The inner voice is never an excuse. It is only a guide.

But what a guide. If we listen to it, we can grow in every way. No more reliance on the input of others to get a sense of self. No more seeking advice to move forward. Begone, cursed insecurity! At long last we are self-reliant, able to trust ourselves and be intimate with our own standards and tastes. (The inner voice is discussed throughout this book. See especially "Hearing Your Inner Voice" and "Handling Criticism," both in chapter seven.)

Patience: Tolerance for time. With patience, we work until our inner voice says a piece is complete, not until we (read: our ego) *want* it to be complete. No longer are we indentured to the alarm clock in our heads that rings, *You're taking too long! Finish it now!* Patience has tossed that alarm clock out the window and in its place wound up a new one that rings only when our work is ready.

Most beginning writers believe that effort equals product, that six days of work (or two months, or whatever arbitrary time frame they select) equals a final story. When the reality of long gestation fails to meet their fantasy of immediate completion, they get frustrated to the point of exasperation and laziness and experience a whole host of negative emotions: feelings of failure, feelings of inferiority, shame. Experienced writers, however, know that effort does not equal a final story as much as it equals getting closer to a final story. They know that while six days of work *may* generate a completed, ready-to-submit manuscript, it's more likely that six days of work will equal a draft—

maybe a great draft, but still a draft. They know they must *consciously* impose an attitude of patience upon themselves, so that when they feel that familiar surge of *Finish it now!* they can counteract it by telling themselves (out loud and repeatedly, if necessary), *What's the hurry? Relax. Take all the time you need.*

Patience is the green card to the state of trying. With it in our wallets, we can try as long as we want, leaving only when we have achieved (or surpassed) our artistic goals, not when some capricious visa expires. Patience changes us as people. It makes us into a Sisyphus with hope: Instead of daily rolling our rock to the top of the hill only to have it tumble back to the bottom, and then steaming with envy over how *other* people's rocks *never* seem to roll back down, patience lets us catch our tumbling rock, every day a little farther from the bottom, until at last we lodge the rock comfortably at the top. Patience conveys our work from the mediocre to the OK to the good to the knock-your-socks-off. It is the smelting of urgency into tranquility, a leisurely renovation of our imperfections, a monument to our self-belief.

With patience, a solution that eludes us one day will come the next—and then the *next* day, an even better solution will come. This is what I found as I wrote my novel, a process that I thought of as crawling through tunnels in a cave: As I inched through twisting, dead-end shafts, over and over I would discover, just as I reached an impasse, some small chink to my side that was worthy of a peek. I would glance through this chink and behold just beyond it a whole new room with vivid colors and rich echoes, and then I'd whip out my pickax and start chipping out a shaft to get there. Once inside, I'd search for a new shaft to keep moving forward. Soon I saw that I could not dig a clear narrative—and certainly never reach my novel's climax—without thousands and thousands of such attempts, each one leading to a new shaft, then a room, a shaft, a room, until I finally got to where I wanted to be.

When writers are trying to produce a story that won't work, many of them end up wailing, "What's wrong with me? What don't I have? I know: It's talent. I just don't have any talent." Almost always the reply could be, "You've got talent. What you lack is patience." But that would be too easy; they wouldn't be able to believe it. "No, I should be better by now," they'd retort. Oh yeah? And Elvis should have come right after Bach, the Wright Brothers should have gone immediately from pacifiers to propellers, and the Roman empire should have sprung up the day after the dinosaurs died.

Evolution is not instantaneous. To be a writer is to be constantly evolving. If anything "should" happen fast, it is not getting the writing done, but accepting that writing takes time.

Physical Exercise: Sustained exertion of our bodies. Most of us spend our days on our butts, our bodies no more than fleshy sacks that contain our minds; we fuel them just enough to keep going and recoil at the thought of lavishing them with any attention that is nonsexual. We know this inactivity is at the expense of our figure, but we have our priorities. And since all we need are our hands and brain, why bother with anything that won't get our books written?

Physical exercise, though, *does* get books written. Forget our figure. Regular physical exercise gives us a structured and reliable path to reverie, and reverie, when allowed to persist for thirty to ninety minutes, can give us solutions to many previously unsolvable literary problems.

This works most effectively with exercise that is aerobic and primarily solitary: walking, running, swimming, biking, even dancing at home. When we are breathing at an increased rate, and our endorphins are applauding, we cannot help but make new mental associations. Aha! We are treating the character of the boss the way we treated our mother! We must rip apart our linear structure and restructure like a symphony! We see the perfect title on the billboard before us!

Thus, as exercise loosens our bodies up, it also invites contemplativeness and nimble-mindedness.

But exercise seems too basic a tool. Surely, we tell ourselves, sneakers mildewing in the corner, if we need a tool at all it should be something more dramatic—more literary—than a morning constitutional. Like alcohol. Or cigarettes, especially arcane brands, maybe clipped into a slender black holder. Or parties, where we can one-up the witticisms of our fellow artists. Or we need a muse, a darling little prodigy who will descend into our dreams and whisper sweet bons mots into our straining and receptive ears. Look at Hemingway. Faulkner. *They* didn't have to join a gym or even stroll around the block. So why should we?

Because it works. And because exercise will keep us living, and hence writing, longer.

Risk/Fun: Daring to step beyond convention—and to do so with excitement. When we begin writing, we usually believe in myths perpetuated by the media: that writers are somber intellectuals who unanimously agree that only certain subjects and styles are worthy, who develop question-mark posture while curled over manuscripts in an attic, whose trousers have holes because new pants cost too much, who announce that writing is *Work, hard work*. A gift. The supreme sacrifice.

So we tell ourselves that we too must develop creased brows, and wince when we read stories that aren't subtle, or experimental, or set in Seattle, or whatever the current preferences appear to be. We must work within these strictures and go no further. We must restrict what we write, how we write, and how we feel about writing. If we have other thoughts, we must keep them away from ourselves. They are not right. They are not honorable. Clip away all those ringlets of inappropriate ideas. Suppress all those high kicks of inappropriate style. Smother that cheer. Writing is not cheer; it is *serious business*. Do not laugh. Do not revel. Get stern. Clear your throat a lot. Skydive only in your dreams. Then, we can mummify ourselves into the shape of a writer, and then maybe eventually the world will come to believe that we are.

But maybe it won't. And if all that self-limitation doesn't result in the recognition we crave, we'll end up spending our lives being someone we are not.

What if, however, we decide to forget the myth? What if we let ourselves enjoy writing as much as we enjoy a double scoop of ice cream with fudge chunks and jimmies, or a day reading a best-seller at the beach? What if we defy the stipulations that we think are out there and simply *do what we want*? And *be who we are*? What if, instead of carving ourselves up into a facsimile of someone else, we buff ourselves up so we're simply more *we*?

We'll have a better time. We'll stop feeling so emotionally congested. Maybe we'll even write something unique, be the maverick whom other people then fashion into myth.

A friend of mine once met Margaret Mead. My friend was ten, Mead in her seventies. The anthropologist-writer had just given a lecture at the local university, and my friend's professor father had invited Mead to the family farm for dinner. I asked my friend, "What was she like?" imagining a walking stick, black cape, solemn pronouncements. And my friend replied, "She threw off her shoes and ran out into the wildflowers, giggling and jumping in the mud. She was freer and happier than any adult I'd ever seen."

By letting ourselves take risks and have fun, we make the journey of writing exciting. And that in turn helps us commit, and embrace discipline, and lock onto the call letters of our inner voice, and delight in our tenacity. Risk/fun pries our writing away from the dust and shadows and sets it out in the sun by the pond. It is our license to drive off the road while squealing *Wheeee!* It is the birthday cake we give ourselves every day of the year.

As Cynthia Heimel wrote once in the *Village Voice*, "When in doubt, make a fool of yourself. There is a microscopically thin line between being brilliantly creative and acting like the most gigantic idiot on earth. So what the hell, leap."

Tenacity: Hanging in there, no matter what. We take many blows as writers. Our story gets rejected by editors. Our novel gets broadsided by reviewers. Interviewers ignore us. We tell ourselves there is no hope—we'll never get published, or if we're published, we'll never get recognition—that somehow our name will forever be written in invisible ink. It is a curse put on our family in the old country, bad karma we earned by jilting a pal in second grade, just another indication of our cosmic role as schlemiel. We are wasting our time. People are laughing at us.

These thoughts are hard to resist, especially if they resemble thoughts that assailed us at other times in our lives. Perhaps when we were younger, we were repeatedly chosen last for the kickball team, or we saw the tenth grader we coveted making goo-goo eyes at someone else, or we raced home with a 98 percent on our arithmetic quiz and got scolded for the single misplaced decimal point in Question 3. On the other hand, perhaps we had few external troubles but suffered with moodiness or moments of melancholy. Either way, many of us spent at least some part of our earlier years asking ourselves if we would ever amount to anything. Sometimes we felt certain we would. Other times we insisted to ourselves that we wouldn't. But when those old thoughts return—the same ones we had in the school corridor at fourteen—their familiarity makes them all the harder to dismiss, regardless of whether their logic is fallacious. It's like an old pop tune we never cared for: If we hear even a snippet of the chorus on the radio, we may reflexively switch stations with a quick *Yech*, yet over the next few days find ourselves compelled to play the whole insipid song repeatedly in our heads, as well as recall what we were doing and feeling when it was popular.

Some phenomena create thought grooves in our minds that return us to memories and previous feelings. Music is one. Smell, as Proust reminds us, is one. And thought is another.

When times get rough in our writing careers, and we begin thinking negative thoughts about ourselves and the world—refracting our self-image from an OK kind of person to a miserable bum—we can quit writing or we can persevere. Quitting is simple. Then all we have to live with is our bitterness toward the world and disappointment in ourselves and grief at the years we wasted. These seem minor prices to pay when we're in the throes of pessimism. But quitting also means accepting the death of possibility, Pandora slamming the lid just before Hope jumps out. In other words, quitting means committing—to a lousy view of life.

Tenacity, though, means allowing ourselves to stay open. We may still think it likely that we won't get published or noticed by the literary world, but we continue with our work, keeping open a sliver of possibility that we might be wrong. We do this because we don't truly believe that the others who reject or malign us are right. *We* are right. We are good writers, and if we keep going and improving, someday the world might see that.

Tenacity has always been a primary theme in the lives of successful writers. Some historians believe that Plato rewrote the first sentence of *The Republic* fifty times; Virgil needed ten years to write *The Aeneid*; Gustave Flaubert's *Madame Bovary*, which itself required five years of work, was not even begun until Flaubert had written and discarded two other novels; James Joyce's *Ulysses* took eight years to write and countless rejections to get published; Ernest Hemingway rewrote the final page of *A Farewell to Arms* almost forty times; Ted Solotaroff, in his essay "Writing in the Cold: The First Ten Years," reveals that Bobbie Ann Mason submitted twenty stories to *The New Yorker* before one was accepted; Solotaroff adds that Raymond Carver wrote for almost ten years before his first story appeared in print, then persevered another seven before publishing his first book; Harold Brodkey's first novel, *The Runaway Soul,* took thirty-one years of revision between its 1960 book contract and its 1991 publication.

These are just a few of the better-known examples, but every author, even the most obscure, has his or her own stories of tenacity.

Tenacity is a bumpy road, not always easy to find and sometimes easy to lose. Supportive friends and spouses are vital to tenacity, people who can methodically talk us through our despondency and help us realize that we are happier when we write, that writing is for writing, not glory. As soon as we feel like quitting, we need to pick up the phone, talk about our feelings, remember why we write. Then we need to write. Immediately. With abandon. Maybe we should even write something that the rejecters/ignorers will *really* hate. Alchemize our anger into passion.

Recently I attended my first horse show. The highlight was a jumping event, during which young equestrians and their horses sailed through a track of twenty or so wooden gates. Their skill was so mesmerizing, I never considered that any might fail until, halfway through the competition, one rider tumbled to the ground. I thought that meant curtains for her—her fall had earned her so many penalty points that she was clearly out of the running and would no doubt slink back to the stables without delay. Yet the custom that has developed into one of our most oft-used metaphors is, apparently, handled with great dignity in the ring; the rider remounted and continued the course, instantly confronting her fears, reviving her dignity, and earning the audience's respect. Although she *was* out of the running, she became visibly more confident, and we applauded her tenacity after she'd jumped her last gate, finishing the course just like everyone else.

Don't delay. When we feel we are going to lose, we must keep on. We are not in a contest for fame nearly as much as we are in a test of our character.

Writing Friends: Buddies who care about writing—and us. Whether the bond is between actual scribes, like Richard Ford and Raymond Carver, or between an author and someone who simply appreciates literature, like Anne Lamott and her nonwriting librarian friend, whether the friendship becomes publically known, like the one between Maxine Kumin and Anne Sexton, or remains a private, special treasure, like my own friendship with novelist Susan Dundon, writing friends help us face all adversities: the story that won't work, the novel that won't sell, the newspaper profile that caricatures us. And, of course, they understand that peculiar form of tree-falling-in-the-woods aloneness with which all writers are familiar. Writing friends also help us rejoice in our successes and present us with their own successes for us to emulate. They are our companions through thick and thin, the light in our night and the hurray in our day. They give us camaraderie, empathy, someone to call when we get news. They want us to win. And with them around, we feel a little more certain that we *will* win.

It is simple to find writing friends. They're everywhere, from the co-worker who loves books to the fellow student whose stories we admire. Maxine Kumin mentions in her essay "The Care-Givers" that she met Anne Sexton in an adult education poetry workshop, before either of them had published a book; I met my friend Susan Dundon at a writer's conference the spring both of us were publishing our first novels. I have also met writing friends in a cubicle at a job we both despised, in a bookstore restroom where I was brushing my teeth, at a clogged checkout line at the supermarket. Our friend-radar can turn on anywhere, at any time, providing that someone who asks about our writing truly relishes our detailed answer and maybe even offers insights. But we know we've zeroed in on a great prospect if they ask to read our work, and then do so promptly, honestly, respectfully; and, if they are writers, they also show their own work to us, listening closely to our comments.

In addition to all this, a good writing friendship needs to last. This may be self-evident, but some people who are compassionate and faithful in ordinary friendships have trouble sustaining such qualities when it comes to being a writing friend. Their envy may encroach, or their feelings of superiority, or their fear of their own or others' neediness. We begin to see evidence of this when we notice that they are giving us much less encouragement than we are giving them, or that their warmth regularly retreats in the face of their—or our—success, or that they neglect to mention if they've read our story, leaving us to tremble over whether they never picked it up at all or burned it in disgust. If such disappointments occur, it is best to recognize that, while this person may be a great buddy, he may not be the best choice for a writing friend. We might need to have a conversation or two about the disparities and discomforts, and then, if necessary, let the friend go, at least for a while.

Unfortunately, we can't know if our writing friendships will survive for the long haul, but we can take precautions to keep them going. If my writing friends and I ever feel envy toward each other, we discuss it, so we can work on those feelings as a team, both learning from the experience. We try to maintain trust. We speak of each other as mutual helpers. We share both our trepidations and exhilarations.

I treasure my writing friends and let them know it. Whenever I feel a sweep of love toward them, I leave a phone message or write a letter saying how much I value them. I send congratulations cards. I throw parties. My friends are integral to my writing. Without these friends, I would still write, but I wouldn't be as happy about it. And how deeply can anything—even writing—satisfy if it doesn't trigger the pleasure of a shared and genuine smile?

CHAPTER FOUR

THE BIG (AND SMALL) LOGISTICS

You are now familiar with the major emotions that can thwart writers, as well as the general antidotes to the more difficult ones. But there remain issues those antidotes don't cure. Maybe you're a working parent. What good is discipline if your only free time falls between Barney and breakfast? Or you're a single person with prodigious social plans, or a wrung-out student. In these and many other cases, talk of tenacity or patience seems too ethereal; what you need are down-to-earth ways to work out the Big Logistics, and maybe some small logistics as well.

When I began college, I'd already juggled school, friends, and a committed writing schedule for years. I figured I'd handle college with the same ease. But freshman week, as I received each syllabus and assessed my many new time commitments, I grew increasingly apprehensive. Each week, I was to read two books, translate fifty lines of Ovid, write a paper, take ballet, and make solid friendships that would last the rest of my life. But I soon found that Latin required five hours a night; papers, entire afternoons; books, whole weekends. Forget my own writing.

On top of this, I couldn't work in my room. High-ceilinged and north-facing, it retained a chill at all times. But I couldn't find anywhere else that was suitable, either. The library was a bazaar of gossiping bodies; the study rooms down the hall, exhibits of cigarette butts and doughnut boxes.

I had no time, and I had no where.

For weeks I felt like a failure. I worked erratically—an hour on my bed, the school lawn, a chair in a corridor. I lost my coffee virginity.

Scarfed candy. Relegated friendships to the wee hours. Relegated my own writing time to never.

Finally I sought help. Hoping to convince someone that I couldn't handle my four classes, I went to my dean.

"Help!" I wailed as I presented my plight. My *unique* plight, that is; surely no one else was as distressed as I.

The dean said, "You can't drop a class." (*Sadist!* I thought.) "But you *can* go see our study specialist."

I felt more bereft than ever. What could a specialist do—spin me extra hours out of thin air?

But I was too despairing to resist, so I dragged myself to the specialist's office, incredulous and mumbling.

The specialist opened the door into a sunny room. I took a seat across from her, wondering if her pronounced blink was the mark of someone who can truly see time or mere eccentricity. I decided on the latter and launched histrionically into my inventory of adversities. Before I'd gotten far she interrupted. "You just need to regain your sense of control," she said.

"I know," I replied. Though I *didn't* really know; I hadn't thought of it that way before. The problem had been too much work, not too little control of me. Then I caught myself. "Okay, I need control. So how am I supposed to get it?"

"Well," she said, "let's begin with a chart."

She pulled out a pad and made a chart and then she taught me almost all the time and place tips I have used ever since, many of which, I realized, involve attitude rather than action. "They seem so simple," I observed. "They do the job," she replied.

That night I began implementing her ideas, and very soon I felt better. My work no longer trampled over me; I'd tamed it. Actually, I'd tamed myself, seen where I was causing my own chaos, and so brought my anxiety—and hence work—under control.

I completed that semester without a single extension or all-nighter. My friends saw me as magical; I could finish papers a week early, remain calm through finals. But it wasn't magic. I'd simply come to discern why time was escaping me. As a result, I understood myself better, and so gained a confidence with my work that I hadn't felt before.

In the next two sections, I review these time and place tips. Then

I'll address similar irksome issues. By the chapter's end you should understand all about logistics—how a writer can have a life and still manage to write.

FINDING TIME TO WRITE

You want to write—perhaps even burn to write a particular story— yet every day flits by, a montage of wage earning and dish washing and I'm-fine-how-are-yous. At the end of each week, you panic at how yet another seven days have passed and you still haven't gotten around to it. You wish, as if you were a cartoon character, for feet that could see tomorrow approaching and skid you back from the edge, digging you deeply into today. You skim articles on literary stars, hunting for how they manage time. A best-selling lawyer divulges that he gets to the office at 4 A.M. and writes until his secretary shows up. A Pulitzer-winning poet discusses her sixty-minute sonnets written when the baby is asleep.

You wonder if you can be so disciplined. Then another week of musts and want-to's passes, and you conclude that you cannot. They must be better people than you, or *you* are better, because you clearly have more friends and interests than they.

Productivity or popularity. How can you choose a few hours of brain pain and dictionary delving over family and friends who are waiting, forks erect, anecdotes bursting to be shared? Maybe those who have less can make that choice. But you just *can't.*

This way of thinking is as silly as mine when I was a freshman. *Everyone* is as busy as you. But some people want to write so badly that they figure out ways to make time. Perhaps they consult with someone. Or they read a book on time management. All that matters is that they do it.

These people are not geniuses. They just recognize that they want to write. Period. Then they take it from there.

In other words, the only requirement to handling this and other logistical issues is drive. *If you want to write badly enough, you will find a way to work out the logistics.*

First, reread the section on "Discipline" in chapter three. Then find a time management process that works for you. You might want to try the approach I learned my freshman year: Make a chart, like the one on the next page, of every waking hour in your week.

Don't fuss if your day begins at 6 P.M. instead of 6 A.M. Just put all your waking hours into this visual form, whatever your rising hour might be. Next, blacken the times when you have responsibility for other matters, such as work, child care, school, worship. Then look at the remaining space, the "free" time when you can possibly write. Obviously, the fewer obligations you have, the more space you will retain, but even with many obligations, you can almost always find a spare hour here or there.

The next step is to commit yourself to a certain number of writing hours per week. I ask beginning writers to commit to a minimum of seven. Even young mothers with children and careers can usually do this. Perhaps when they examine their charts, they see a free hour every night after the baby is asleep. More likely, they see that three times a week they can find 2¼ hours, or 3½ hours twice a week. I've worked with someone who could fit her hours in only if she rose at four and wrote until six. Since this was grueling, the seven-hour requirement made the chore less onerous, since it meant that she rose before the birds only every other day. I've also worked with people whose business trips eliminated the possibility of sticking to the same seven hours each week. They simply made a new chart every Monday, figuring it out fresh each time.

Juggle it around until you can fit in your seven hours.

When you can manage more, you win the gold star. The ideal amount of writing time is three or four hours a day. Start with seven hours a week and then, down the road, try ten. If you can do that, go up to fourteen. Eventually, see if you can get to an hour count somewhere between twenty-one and twenty-eight.

Yes, this time does add up. *Any* amount of time adds up. It is said that in the seventeenth century, French Chancellor D'Aguesseau, whose wife arrived ten minutes late for dinner every evening, used that time to write. After a year, he had written a book, which then became a best-seller.

You may not write a best-seller with ten-minute writing sessions. But I guarantee you that if you consistently put in seven-hour weeks, you will make tremendous progress with your work. To ensure that you stay on track, keep a log of your hours. (Refer to "Process Journal" in chapter six.) Be honest. And include how you felt during

Time	Mon.	Tues.	Wed.	Thurs.	Fri.	Sat.	Sun.
6 A.M.							
7 A.M.							
8 A.M.							
9 A.M.							
10 A.M.							
11 A.M.							
12 P.M.							
1 P.M.							
2 P.M.							
3 P.M.							
4 P.M.							
5 P.M.							
6 P.M.							
7 P.M.							
8 P.M.							
9 P.M.							
10 P.M.							
11 P.M.							
12 A.M.							

each session. This will help you to know yourself better as you learn how to reconceive your options with time.

It sounds elementary, and it is. But it works.

What if, however, you have trouble fitting in your full seven hours? Or what if you want to wedge in more hours a week but can't figure out how? This is where attitude comes in.

Setting Priorities

For each obligation in your chart, ask yourself if you absolutely must do it. Yes, you need to attend classes and jobs, but must you go to every PTA meeting? Could you watch less TV? Are you required to eat lunch with your co-workers every day?

Some writers skip their favorite activities for a while. Or they recognize that, though they love Tuesday dinners with their friend Margaret or the daily *Times* crossword puzzle, they love writing more and so reduce the frequency of those other pleasures.

Examine every obligation and ask yourself if it's as important to you as writing. If it's the same, or if it's *truly* an obligation and not a desire, try to decrease the time you put in. For instance, weeknight hours can be saved if you prepare your lunches on Sunday. Lifetimes are won if dishes pile up a few times a week. As for meetings—go late, or leave early.

Trim everything you can.

Travel Time

Think about how you get around physically. In the car, we can write only at stoplights and in traffic jams. But on trains, buses, and planes, we can write throughout the trip. Since a lot of our time is spent in transit, see if you can take public transportation more often so you can create an opportunity to write. Or see if you can carpool and write in the back seat.

However, writing during transit works only if you resist talking with fellow passengers. This can be trying since many people look to others for entertainment during their journeys. I've sat beside strangers who, when they couldn't ensnare me in chitchat, spent the entire six-hour train ride staring into space. I find it foolish to squander such time, but that's their choice. Unless they're your own kids, other people's recreation is none of your business. (This includes car pools.) If a talk-famished person sits near you when you've planned on writing, just write. Most people will leave you alone. If they don't, simply keep your eyes on the paper and say, "I can't talk. I have work to do." Say it until they give up.

Also, recognize that when you feel coerced by other people's expectations, you're probably oppressing yourself more than they. One of my students, a woman with grown children, planned to write during a long plane ride. Assigned to an empty row, she boarded in anticipation of writing bliss. But just as the plane was about to take off, two last-minute passengers got on: a young mother and her infant. They were seated beside my student, who instantly became unglued: The young mother would want help, of course. She'd want strangers tickling Junior's chin and offering to fetch the flight attendant and who knows what else. My student seethed over these demands, but still pulled out her laptop and did her work. When she told me this story, I asked if the young mother had actually made any requests. No. Had she seemed in need of help? No. Had she made a single gesture in your direction? No. So why had my student lavished so much energy on this imaginary conflict? Because she'd projected her own feelings from when *she* was a young mother. Those feelings were hers, not the woman's beside her. In the end, my student did the right thing, but she needn't have endured such agony to do it. The only interference came from her.

Remember boundaries: where your feelings stop and someone else's start. They are separate. You may need to tell yourself this consciously, over and over. Maintaining boundaries is a terribly important part of taking care of yourself as a writer. (Refer to "Boundaries," chapter three.)

Asking for Help

See if other people in your life can help. You may well lack time because you do for others what they can do for themselves. This is often true of women, especially those in families. With housework on the left, a job on the right, and kids in between, most women can't see any time, let alone seven hours a week.

But they could if others in the household helped. This might mean that a couch potato husband must wash the dishes three times a week or that children take care of their own laundry.

Such requests are not easy to make of one's family, who are accustomed to the status quo. Kids refuse to clean the tub. Spouses won't empty the trash. Moms are expected to do all.

Though you may not realize it, you may have contributed to this situation by your attitude. Many of us believe that others' needs are greater than our own and that this applies *every moment*. We never give ourselves the attention we give our spouses or children or friends, forgetting where our own feelings start because we never let others' feelings stop; we feel their blues and their highs to such an extent that we let them wash away our own feelings. (The psychological term for this is *codependence*, which means valuing other people's feelings more than our own to the point where our sense of worth comes only through others, and we look to others to define us.) The result of this behavior is that others see us as need-free. It becomes as inconceivable to them that we could have needs as it is to us that we might verbalize those needs.

If you need assistance from your family, sit them down, individually or as a group, and tell them you have new needs now. Then state what you need and how they can help, offering to teach. "Lucy, I need you to cook on Monday nights. This is my tuna recipe." "James, I want you to take the bus to your drum lessons. Let's see how to read the schedule together." Try this a week or two, and if it doesn't work, come up with some other solution. "Here's money to get a pizza." "Here's money to take a taxi." Again, if this doesn't work, try a different approach. Your options are only as limited as your creativity.

If you feel uncomfortable making these requests, then examine why. Are you nervous they won't like you? Do you believe they can't take care of themselves? Have you always had trouble communicating your needs? Try to find the cause, and then either reread the relevant sections in this book or go to a store to find books that address it. Maybe you feel you're not assertive enough. Then go to the Self-Help or Psychology sections of your bookstore and leaf through the books on assertiveness. Maybe you feel you won't be able to control their diet. Then you might benefit from reading books on letting go.

Maybe, however, you can't make requests because your family *is* truly helpless—you have a disabled spouse or no spouse and an active toddler. If so, get help. Pay someone to take over while you write, or see if a community group can provide respite care. Call social service agencies to see what they offer.

If all else fails, sneak in a few minutes a day to write about your frustration in a journal. When the frustration gets acute, you'll probably find yourself with a turbocharged resolve to make some changes. Then you'll cram in those hours one way or another, because you'll so desperately want to.

Acceptance

Accept that sometimes it hurts.

A writer working on her first novel, a mystery set in North Carolina, is constantly steeped in rage. She quit her job to write full-time while her husband supported her, but soon thereafter he injured himself on his own job. Though not debilitating, the resulting impairment forced him into early retirement. So instead of having her days alone, the writer suddenly had a spouse around who didn't know what to do with himself. She moved her desk to the attic for privacy, yet every day her husband found some reason to come up. "I made tea. Let's drink it under the willow." Or "I'm going to the store. Will you come for company?" The writer would steam over the intrusion—but she would comply every time! So she got no writing done and found a lot more gray in her hair.

As Ann Landers says, "No one can take advantage of you without your permission." You have the option of telling people, "Not until I'm done at five." Or, "I can't go shopping now." Or even, "I won't answer your knock when I'm writing. I can't."

The writer knew all this but couldn't bring herself to implement it, because "then I'll look selfish." Her friends pointed out that her husband's behavior was selfish. "That doesn't matter. It still makes me feel bad." Her therapist explained that she and her husband are separate beings. Her time is her time; his is his. If he can't find a way to occupy himself during her writing hours, that's not her fault or responsibility. "I know," she told her therapist. "But it still feels bad."

This brings us to the real hard part: Sometimes it feels bad. We might know that we're doing the right thing by saying no to someone we love, but we feel like jerks for doing it.

There is only one way to push yourself through this. Accept that you feel bad, but press on. Tell yourself—a thousand times a day, if necessary—that your time is *your* time, and your desire to write is important. Tell yourself that you do not blend into anyone else and that, while they might treat you as extensions of themselves, you do not have to go along with that. Reread the sections in chapter three on boundaries and commitment. Retrain how you think about your-self. After all, your self-image is shifting from nonwriter to writer. So it's not that great a leap for it to change in other ways as well.

The writer in my example has still not completed her North Carolina mystery, but she has acquired an ulcer.

The Right Time

If you can't make time now, you have two choices. Either you do not have a strong enough yearning to be a writer, or this is not the time for you to write. If it's the former, put this book down now and get on with your life. If it's the latter, do any extra-writing activities you can: read books, befriend writers, attend readings, and, most impor-tantly, write letters or keep a journal. It's helpful just to be in a state where you dream onto the page; then, when your life gets less hectic, your writing muscles will be in fairly good shape.

If, however, you feel for years that this is not the time to write, ask yourself if that is really true, or if you are using it as an excuse for writer's block, insecurity, laziness, etc. Then refer to those sections in this book.

FINDING WHERE TO WRITE

I once read a fascinating study on romance novelists. It said that most romance authors are homemakers who come to writing from a background of Band-Aids and bouillon and a pure love of romance novels. When they begin to write, their families, so used to seeing them as "just Mom," chuckle at the absurdity of her needing any private space. So most of the romance writers in this study penned their first novel on pads they carried around in their aprons. Passionate kisses in moonlit gardens were scribbled in the kitchen as gravy simmered on the stove; heartbreaking confessions in sump-tuous restaurants were jotted down in the bathroom as the kids splashed in the tub; poetic proposals on galloping stallions were scrawled at the table as the family ate dinner. Not until these women published their first novel did they gain their family's respect—and hence "win" their own privacy: a countertop or maybe a desk.

The study presented me with stories of unshrinking determination. Each of these women wanted to write her book, and write it she would, despite having no place of her own.

The logistical problem of location applies to all writers, particularly in beginning stages of their careers. Raymond Carver, in an interview with Michael Schumacher, admits that in his early writing days, when he had a bunch of young children and no secluded space in his house, he would steal away from all the chaos to write in his car. Not that he'd drive somewhere picturesque; he'd simply climb into the car and sit in the parking lot and write. It was the only place available to him where he knew he could find quiet.

Not all writers need to improvise so dramatically. When I was a teenager trying my first novel, I washed my hair every night, then sat in the kitchen beneath my mother's salon-style hair dryer, the kind with the big heated head-bowl. It took half an hour to dry my hair, so every night I had that time to write. Since I couldn't hear anyone, no one could bother me. I wrote a whole novel this way.

To be honest, I didn't *have* to sit under the dryer to get privacy. I had my own room, so theoretically I could have written there. But I had learned that my writing space had to meet two requirements: absolute quiet, which I couldn't get in a room so close to my sister's Three Dog Night albums; and dedicated purpose, which I couldn't get in a room that served as my study hall and a hangout for my friends. Under the hair dryer, I had utter silence and a location where all I did was write. These two requirements still determine my work space. Some years ago I moved out of a noisy city so I could find a quiet house in the suburbs. Then I angled my desk so I split the room in two—the writing part and the dress/sleep/socialize part.

If you try different ways of handling space, you'll eventually learn what's right for you. A friend of mine *needs* noise to write, so she works in cafes. A widely published essayist keeps a bed in his office, because he likes to write lying down. Benjamin Franklin is said to have done much of his writing in his bathtub. John Cheever is well known for having made a daily ritual of descending the elevator of his apartment building to a windowless room in the basement, where he hung up his jacket and did his writing. A graduate of a prestigious M.F.A. program wrote a good chunk of his master's thesis at two in the morning while scrunched up in the phone booth at the end of his dormitory hallway. In college, I found I did calculus best in the Pizza Hut, anthropology best in the geology study, and everything else best in the basement of the library, which the gabby masses avoided because of the absence of windows and the abundance of boxes. I also learned that, while I had to write my first drafts away from my room, I could easily type and revise them when I returned.

Be creative. Experiment to discover what works for you.

Here are a few tips I have learned.

Public Spaces—Free

• *Libraries.* I live in libraries when I'm writing first drafts. Except to eat and answer the call of nature, I can sit for days. But by "library," I don't just mean the local public variety (newer public libraries are generally one large room—one large *noisy* room where sound travels well). I also mean nearby college, law, and medical school libraries, which often allow outsiders to use carrels. Call the Circulation Department and ask about the policy. I also use private libraries. These are sometimes affiliated with museums; historical, philosophical, and ethical societies; architectural collections; and professional schools. Some ask for an entrance fee; some require an annual membership. You can find these by looking through the *American Library Directory*, which lists every library in the United States, including hours. Also, see Lee Ash and William G. Miller's *Subject Collections*, which arranges all U.S. public, private, and government libraries in terms of subject collections. Both of these resources are available at most public libraries.

• *Your Office.* Some employers do not want employees on the premises during off-hours. Others are accommodating. (Sometimes saying you're doing homework, rather than writing, wins you the permission you require.) A word of caution: If you work on a company computer, save your work on a disk that you keep at home.

• *Bookstores.* Many large bookstores have both random seating and espresso bars. In either you can write for hours without staff intrusion. The disadvantage to bookstores is that, like the next three categories, they usually pipe in music.

• *Hotel Lobbies.* Most hotels leave you alone if you sit quietly. I don't use them on a daily basis, but if I have time between appointments, hotel lobbies are almost as nice as a library.

• *Train and Bus Stations.* Good people-watching. Usually heated and air-conditioned.

• *Shopping Malls.* Often, you can find an empty seat in the public areas.

• *Parks.* Useful only in nice weather, though some have indoor spaces.

Public Spaces—Some Charge

- *Cafes and Coffeeshops.* Great for atmosphere, and most provide free refills.
- *Restaurants/Diners.* One year I did all my writing at a diner near my job. I took a late lunch at 3 P.M., sat in the far corner, ordered a roll and coffee, and wrote. Because that is a dead time for waiters, the staff left me alone without getting grumpy.
- *Trains and Buses.* A teacher of mine bought writing space by paying her bus fare, then riding to the far end of the line and back. Some transit systems demand additional fare; others don't.

If you write in a public place, avoid times of peak density. For eating establishments, that's mealtimes; for hotel lobbies, convention weekends; for public libraries, afternoons at the ends of school semesters.

Also, places that seem crowded sometimes possess secret seats in quiet areas. I mentioned above that I coped with my busy college library by finding peace in the basement. Users of public spaces tend to gravitate toward windows and distraction. If you look for seats that are more tucked away, you might just find your ideal writing spot. (But bear in mind that crime sometimes occurs in secluded areas. Know your environment.)

Private Spaces

- *Your Own Apartment/House.* This works only if you can concentrate there. Possible complications are that you lack room; your family refuses to cooperate; you can't find any place where you feel comfortable.

If you lack room, consider using one of the public spaces listed above, or seeing if anything can be rearranged in your home. Do you need the sewing machine out all the time or just when you sew? Or use the furniture differently. If the desk is covered with bills, use the dining room table or washing machine. Be creative.

If your family or housemates won't cooperate—they barge into your room, play loud music, monopolize the computer—again, move to a public space or experiment. If doors don't keep them out, try a lock, or a shopkeeper's cardboard clock: "Don't interrupt until 10:00." If they blast the stereo, trade two hours of silence for a ride to the mall, or tune your radio to a spot between stations where you hear nothing but a white noise hiss, or wear earplugs. If they won't share the computer, pay them for the time or rent your own computer. Keep your boundaries clear and try everything.

If, though, after all this, you still don't feel comfortable in your own home, you have two options. One is—yes, again—go to a public space. The other is to examine why you are blocked. See chapter eight for more insight on this.

• *Other People's Houses.* During the summers, a novelist I know house-sits for a friend. Though the friend is indeed out of town at that time, she doesn't need a house-sitter, nor does the novelist need a place to live. But he does need a study away from home, as he has small children. So during the summers, Daddy has a job: He packs his lunch, commutes by rail to "house-sit," writes all day, and at 5 P.M. he heads home.

Sometimes friends or relatives can provide similar assistance. Maybe they work days and you don't, so you can use their place then. Or they travel on weekends or have a spare bedroom in which you can work any time. However you arrange things, when others are involved, it is important to keep them happy. Offer money or barter for cleaning/cooking services. You might also want to suggest that you put the agreement in writing. Then they can be sure that you would make good if anything should happen to their property.

BALANCING WRITING AND EXTRA-WRITING ACTIVITIES

Forget all these time and place logistics. You've got them worked out. Indeed, you are so on your way that you have immersed yourself in the writing world. You attend readings and participate in a writing group. And lately you've discovered a whole wealth of extra-writing activities, activities you can't bring yourself to say no to: writing reviews, tutoring for a literacy program, reading for a magazine, editing an anthology. . . .

And suddenly you see that you don't have a moment to write.

This squashing out of writing by extra-writing activities happens when our excitement for the latter overtakes our enthusiasm for the former. After all, it's rewarding to feel part of a community, to nurture writers, to feel valuable. It seems much more stimulating than other social interactions, and is certainly more fun than flailing through our own literary logjams. And behind-the-scenes activities can make us *feel* like writers, even when they keep us from getting any writing done.

Virtually no writer avoids this pickle. It's almost inevitable; writing is so solitary that, ultimately, everyone who does it tries to find others of like mind. This leads to groups, classes, organizations, meetings, conferences; to finding gratification in extra-writing deeds. At some point or other, most writers get sucked into doing too many of them, or too much of one, at the expense of their own writing.

Sometimes we are able to maintain a comfortable balance. Maybe we were happily writing three hours a day, and then, to broaden our literary windshield, we volunteered to teach writing in the state prison, edit a newsletter for our food co-op, judge a library poetry contest. The balance seems acceptable if we can keep up our three hours a day with ease, or if we reduce our writing time but find we are writing much better.

Sometimes, however, the balance becomes unacceptable. A friend of mine, while struggling to finish a collection of stories, started a reading series. In between my first two books, I critiqued any manuscript that friends and fans sent me, which was a considerable amount. My friend and I both plunged into our new responsibilities with gusto, delighted to be of service to other writers. In time, however, we saw that we couldn't get our work done. With its PR duties and continuous quests for original voices, the reading series yanked my friend up from her desk whenever she sat down. As for me, I found myself with stacks of novels spilling like oil slicks across my days. My friend and I grew surly and snappy, blocked and impatient, resentful and self-loathing, all because we neglected to balance our writing and our extra-writing. That is, we forgot that we had the power to tell ourselves no.

Often, the inability to say no to ourselves is another version of the inability to say no to others. Part of why I kept reading those manuscripts was that people asked me to—you could even say *expected* me to. I told myself it was good for me, but in truth, it was usually good for them and a pain in the ass for me. My friend with the reading series told herself that it was as important to help other writers as it was to write. But in truth, she was giving others more importance than herself.

To say no to yourself, first discern if you need to say no to others. (See sections on "Boundaries" in chapter three and "Finding Time to Write" in this chapter.)

Next, recognize that the process of saying no to yourself breaks down into two developments: You have to not-want whatever you are refusing, and you have to implement that not-want.

How do you decide if you should want or not-want? I don't feel, as you might assume, that writing should always take priority. As Ecclesiastes says: To every thing there is a season. At certain times, we're more able to feed our souls if we're writing. At other times, we benefit more from being out in the world.

When I look back to the time of the torrent of manuscripts, I know that, while part of my problem was that I couldn't say no to others, the remaining part was that I was despondent. My romantic life was ailing; my book sales hadn't met my most meager expectations; I hated where I lived. I needed a break from my computer, since all I did at the keyboard was sulk. My friend began her writing series at a less vulnerable time, but she was trying to come up with new stories, and her head had come to feel opaque whenever she faced a blank page.

Sometimes, when our personal lives are shaken up—we're acquiring a new love, we're suffering from lost love, we're recovering from the joys and disappointments of grad school, we're recovering from the joys and disappointments of publication, we're giving birth to our children, we're comforting someone who's ill or dying—we find we cannot keep our writing concentration. When that happens, we might need to tip the scales in favor of being away from the desk and completely immersed in our lives. We might even feel we have no choice.

Similar measures may also be called for when our creative imaginations seem to be growing rickety and predictable, that is, when we can't come up with ideas that are any different from those we've already written, let alone ideas that are more developed. This sometimes occurs when we have written a story that was so well received by our friends and/or the public that we cannot see past the successful plot, structure, style, etc. It blocks our vision and clogs our process. Our comfort with risk becomes tentativeness; our thoughts approach aridity. (See "Risk/Fun" in chapter three and "Writing—the Tough Stuff" in chapter ten.) Again, we might find that we need to take a break from writing.

In both these cases—major life transitions and writing after a success has stamped an imprint on us—we probably want to maintain some connection to our love of writing but want to do so without actually producing. So we invite our new lover to accompany us to literary readings instead of asking her to sit beside our computer while we write, or we accept an editing job while our newborn sleeps in his crib instead of trying to cozy up to our own revisions. Almost by definition, we then get into an imbalance between writing and extra-writing. But it is not a harmful imbalance; this imbalance, coming out of necessity as it does, is temporarily acceptable.

Unacceptable balances are the trouble. They occur when we have regained our concentration or regalvanized our imaginations but find we now have all these new extra-writing obligations and no longer wish to fulfill them. Eventually my depression subsided, but by then I was drowning in my self-inflicted slush pile. My friend's reading series sent her ideas soaring but enmeshed her free hours so thoroughly that she could not weave those ideas into words.

However we first introduce extra-writing activities into our lives, balance is rarely a problem at first. If it becomes unacceptable at all, that occurs over time, the result of our own growth and/or the demands on us increasing.

My friend and I went through months of frustration before we realized we needed to make a change. By then our new commitments were deeply etched into our lives. We were lucky, though: We recognized that in writing, as in most of life, it is rarely too late to change something that has ceased to work well for us; only our own fears and codependent tendencies prevent us from taking the necessary, positive steps.

So how did my friend and I remedy our respective tilts?

First, we reestablished our sense of boundaries, which we both learned about through a combination of therapy and trial and error. Second, we bribed ourselves. My friend cut the chains of the reading series by finding and splitting the duties with a partner and then doing her share only during the summer, when her writing gets sluggish anyway. (The bribe: the end of guilt over not writing during her most difficult time of the year.) I thinned the pile of manuscripts by giving myself the rule that I would no longer look at work unless it belonged to a close writing friend—or, if from strangers, I charged money. (The bribe: actual moolah, which then paid my rent and which, in fact, led me to start teaching private classes.)

If you find yourself suffering from an unacceptable balance between writing and extra-writing (or other social) activities, ask yourself the basic question of whether you *really* want to write. If the answer is yes, then trace the history of your actions. How long have they felt unbalanced? How did this start? How have you grown since then? Have the duties multiplied? Do you still need the therapeutic effects of the extra-writing activities? Then go through the process I discussed above and juggle, bribe, cut back, or cut loose.

But let's say that, when you ask yourself if you *really* want to write, you answer, "Sort of," and admit that you generally prefer extra-writing activities to writing. If so, then relish your position. The world needs organizers, editors, tutors, and all kinds of extra-writer characters. They need just as much skill and tenacity as writers and are just as essential for the survival of literature.

So when you are feeling stuck in an unacceptable balance, ask yourself which side of the scale you genuinely feel yourself to be on. If it's writer, then unload the necessary pounds from the opposite side until the adjustments feel right. If it's extra-writer, then don't worry about achieving a perfect horizontal between the two sides; a diagonal will do just fine.

Because the goal isn't fame, or wealth, or realized dreams. The goal is learning who you are and fine-tuning the balance so you can let that self be.

FINDING MONEY

You love writing so much that your fingers feel incomplete when away from the keyboard. Every minute you dream of new sentences. Time is words; words are your life. You wish you could hoard time, buy time, *own* time so you could scribble up and down and across it as much as you goddamn pleased.

But you can't; you've got no trust fund or benefactor. It's the greatest tragedy of fate that you've got to work to eat. You hope that you sell a book for six figures, but you also recognize that most first books of fiction get advances of $10,000 or less. So how are you going to fill your plate on a regular basis and still get in your time for writing?

Writers have agonized over this for centuries. In our time, a minuscule number of authors lives in affluence, but the huge majority of writers earns almost nothing from their craft. (A recent survey by the Princeton Survey Research Associates on behalf of the Author's League Fund found that fiction, nonfiction, and drama authors earned a median income of $3,058 per year, based on an average of twenty-six hours of writing a week.) In my own writing career, I've had years when I fell into pots of gold, and years when I earned less than $3,500 (and one year less than $600!). For a long time I managed to live on this, but I had no mortgage, no children, no savings, no vacations, no car, no new shoes, no orchestra tickets, no sprees or splurges, no retirement fund.

Living on money earned from writing means living for the short run. You cannot make comfortable, long-term financial plans if you obtain your money exclusively from writing.

"Wait," you say. "I just read about some young socialite author who got $500,000 for her first book!"

Right. But first, notice that the socialite's advance was deemed worthy of reporting. That's because it's as rare as a singing donkey. Second, do your math. After her agent takes a cut (usually 15 percent), and the government takes its, the socialite will have lost at least a third to a half of her advance if not more. And, though a few hundred thousand dollars still sounds good, there are no guarantees that the socialite will repeat the coup. She might be unable to write ever again (writer's block, used up her material, etc.), or this book, despite its advance, might flop, deterring an editor from offering such a generous advance in the future.

So unless you're writing something remarkably trendy that nets a dazzling advance and is well hyped, *and* lightning strikes, you won't live prosperously on a writer's salary.

I still have trouble accepting this. But since writers must eat, we must find ways to cope.

This is what I do:

Most importantly, I write as much as I can, trying always to have manuscripts around for eager editors.

I write in as many forms as I can. I began my publishing career with short stories, then a novel. I am now working on some personal essays. I have recently begun writing editorials for a city newspaper. And I have worked with movie producers on film treatments, television producers on scripts, and composers on musical adaptations of my work. This way, I keep as many doors open as possible.

I apply for grants. When I win them, they keep me going for six months or a year.

I live inexpensively. I buy clothes in thrift shops, eat vegetarian, return some long-distance calls by letter, cook rather than dine out, rent a room rather than an apartment, and barter whenever I can (I type my hairdresser's school papers; do my accountant's emergency filing).

In the past, when times got tight, I did temporary secretarial work. The pay is pretty good, and I always felt a great deal of respect from my employers because I could word process quickly *and* correct their grammar as I did so.

Then for a few years I taught private writing classes out of libraries, cafes, my dining room, friends' houses (waiving their tuition for the space), etc. The advantage to private teaching over institutional teaching is freedom: I decided when the class began and ended, whom to include, how to teach. Once, when I was teaching at a commuting university, I realized halfway through the semester that I needed to meet with the students more frequently, an impossibility given their many jobs and family responsibilities. My fantasy was that I could turn the class of ten into ten tutorials. But I couldn't, since the students would then lack their credit hours. With my private classes, I could make any alterations—at any time during the course—that the students and I agreed were helpful. Plus, I didn't have to give grades (which, for the most part, I see as a pointless and almost arbitrary exercise for any teacher in the arts).

Sometimes, such as now, I stop my private teaching and switch to teaching at universities. The main advantages to institutional teaching over private teaching are these: a ready supply of students, especially, if the class is an elective, students willing to embrace risk; an environment where self-reflection and challenge are, with luck, the norm; and a steady salary. I also adore having library facilities, and colleagues to whom I can turn for advice and camaraderie.

But if you are thinking of pursuing full-time university teaching to support yourself as a writer, be aware that, although they are emotionally satisfying, creative writing positions are not particularly easy to find, even if you have classroom experience and have published. Also, know that most schools cut their costs by limiting new hires to adjunct teaching, which pays by the course. (In community colleges and state schools, this is usually between $1,500 and $2,500 per course, no benefits. Ivy League schools might pay closer to $4,000 or $5,000 per course.) Universities also stay within their budgets by limiting new teachers to one-year appointments, which for you, the teacher, means an itinerant lifestyle. The upshot of all this is that, until you land in a full-time position, you may have less time to write than you would have expected or less stability than you might require.

What about other kinds of day (or night) jobs?

Recently, I lucked into a great day job. I am the events coordinator at a large bookstore, which means that I seek out authors, musicians, artists, dancers, and knowledgeable speakers to appear in the store; I publicize the events by sending material to and connecting with media people; and I host the events, ensuring that the author, et al., has a good (and, god willing, financially remunerative) time. Almost all large bookstores in the country have this position, which is technically called the Community Relations Coordinator. I have found being a CRC extremely beneficial to my writing career, as it has allowed me to befriend many writers and people in publishing, to establish relationships with the media, to discover the ins and outs of book sales and marketing, and to acquire information on a slew of subjects I would not have otherwise known about. (Just this last month, I learned about posture from a chiropractor, Old English dancing from a dance troupe, Vaclav Havel's plays from a theater company, Native American circle talks from a Cherokee chief, the world of chess from participants in a chess tournament, and what it's like to be an author from writers much further along in their careers than I.) In addition, since I host the events, and the events are mostly at night, I don't need to get to work until two or three o'clock in the afternoon, leaving my mornings free so I can write.

Other pay-the-rent day and night jobs that my friends have had include restaurant work, overnight shifts (copy centers, convenience stores, typing pools, security detail), emergency rooms (only for people with medical training), phone operation, proofreading, copyediting, retail, logging, working on an oil drill, nude dancing. The list of famous writers who did grunt work is endless. Henry Miller dug graves. William Faulkner ran rum. Douglas Unger was a fisherman. Anne Lamott cleaned houses. A marvelous young novelist named Susan Jedren used to drive a delivery truck for a baking goods company. Basically, if you have the training (Rick Bass was a geologist, Amy Bloom is a therapist) and/or are willing to work at hours or perform tasks that other people find undesirable (William Burroughs was an exterminator, Carl Sandburg a janitor), you can find employment that will allow you the time to write. With luck that can even occur while you are on the job: a friend of mine monitors R.E.M.

machines at a sleep lab, which means that for thirty-eight hours of his forty-hour week he can write; I certainly got a lot of writing done while I was temping, filling those hours between memos by typing mounds of new stories.

Sometimes students ask if they should get a job as an editor or newspaper reporter or do technical writing for a business. This can be done; after all, Amy Tan was a technical writer before *The Joy Luck Club*. But the risk is that after a day of writing-related work, you might hit mental burnout by the time you get home and sit down to your own writing. As a result, you may get writing done but, as happens with many of my students who are journalists, less writing than you would like. I recommend to students that they take an editing job if they want to be an editor as well as a writer; but if they want to be a writer, period, and a highly productive one at that, they ought to consider some other source of income, even if that's scooping ice cream, or collecting trash, or fixing cars.

As with the other logistical issues, when it comes to earning money, you need to be creative and try different approaches. Keep your eyes open to possibility. Look at what your friends do and see if it might work for you. I wouldn't have known about CRC work if I hadn't had a friend in that position. Make calls to learn more. Let people know you're interested in hearing their employment ideas. Network (see chapter nine). Skim not just the classified ads in your paper but the business section as well, because there you can read about a wide range of mavericks and entrepreneurs, gleaning inspiration and direction. And take risks. I am currently investigating the possibility of syndicating my editorials, which would mean more money *and* national exposure for the same amount of time that I am already putting in. I don't know that I'll succeed, but it won't hurt me to try. I am also speaking with people I know at radio stations about running an interview program for writers, which would mean meeting more authors and learning more about publishing. Again, I don't know that I'll land such a show, but I might as well give it a try.

Writers are creators. As such, we can be as inventive with our ideas about income as we are with theme, narrative, or characterization. We can limit our writing to the page, or we can write both our writing and our lives.

PART TWO

THE PROCESS

CHAPTER FIVE

THE EDUCATION
OF THE WRITER

We know we want to write. That much is clear. But we recognize that writing is a skill, and, as with all other skills—medicine, piano, baseball, bartending—a certain degree of learning will be necessary. We know what to do to learn *those* skills. If we want to be a doctor, we take a premed curriculum in undergraduate years, study for the MCATs, go to medical school, do our residency, etc. If we want to play piano, we study with a music teacher and practice our fingers off. Baseball we learn from playing on a team; bartending we learn in a class or on the job.

But writing is learned in a myriad of ways. There is no single path that will deposit you conclusively into the glistening Shangri-la of The Successful Career as a Writer. Plus, what works for others may not work for you. Indeed, the path to becoming a good writer is no more clear or universal than the path to becoming a good person. We get to each place through trial and error, through staying the course yet digressing down crooked trails, through keeping our eyes open while keeping our guts willing, through not just trying but trying intelligently.

So, since there is no one way to reach the goal of learning to write, how can you ascertain how best to spend your energies? My students often debate this, declaring at various moments of epiphany that— Eureka! They *now* know what is most vital in learning how to write: "Reading," some assert, thumping their Dickens; "Attending classes," profess others, brandishing college catalogs like pennants; "Finding mentors," argue a few, throwing roses to a published author; "Listening to others," add a handful, scribbling down what everyone else is saying; "Seeing yourself as a writer," proclaims the silent majority, flipping on their computers.

The truth is that, when you are learning how to become a writer, all the above are important. You just need to consider the ins and outs of each, and to make sure you achieve a balance.

In this chapter, I discuss these ways of educating oneself as a writer. The only major activity I won't discuss is the writing itself. The next three chapters will address that in detail.

WHOM AND HOW TO READ

Writers read. They must. Reading provides writers with models of possibility—how to introduce the headmaster in a suspicious way, how to skip suspensefully from the corpse in the garden to the nursemaid rocking her charges, how to walk the reader inside a West Virginia coal mine in such a way that soot seems to line the pages. Reading also provides writers with models of failure: This opening paragraph should be filed under "Sominex"; this parlor is so minutely described that we care more about the bric-a-brac than about our heroine seducing her date on the divan; this bank president's dialogue reads exactly the same as that of the taxi driver and the pigtailed tomboy. Reading, which writer Bob Shacochis has wisely dubbed "the Siamese twin of writing," is the best way beginning writers have to teach themselves and advanced writers have to continue their education.

It is important that you become familiar with both contemporary books and the classics. The former are vital because they are written by your peers in your own time, and because by looking at them you can absorb the range of styles, subject matter, and technical tricks that writers are currently exploring. This way, you can create a mental map of the present literary landscape and discover where both the overexplored and underexplored territories are. The classics are important because they are written by your forebears, and by studying them you can see not only style, subject matter, and technical tricks but also how writers' thought processes and audiences' expectations have changed over time.

Aside from these reasons, writers can benefit from reading both contemporary and classic authors by using them as examples of standards. That is, each story or book is an opportunity for you to ask yourself, What do I think works? What do I think doesn't? What are *my* standards, and do I have this author's talent/gumption to try to reach them?

I do not want to make a specific reading list here, since all writers are unique, and consequently, the precise books that would prove useful are unique as well. But it is not difficult to form your own list. Simply think about what you want to write—literary short stories, horror novels, epic poetry, etc.—and then explore the entire history of that form. Start with contemporary authors. You can do this by reading book reviews and speaking with like-minded readers. I also strongly suggest you spend time in a bookstore doing what librarians call "shelf reading," which means that you patiently look at the spine and perhaps the inside of every book on a particular shelf (in this case, the new books shelf in the area of literature that appeals to you) so you familiarize yourself with what's out there.

Then buy some books and read them. You'll often find that both the inside and the outside of almost any book can provide you with breadcrumbs to lead you to the next destination of another author. Within the text, writers frequently make references (through epigraphs, metaphors, allusions, etc.) to other writers, both contemporary and classic, who influenced them. On the outside of the book, you can examine the blurbs, those superlative quotations on the back cover from famous living writers. Either way, you then have some direction on where to proceed.

In addition, read author interviews, which you might see in a newspaper or magazine, on the Internet, or in the reference books *Current Biography*, *Contemporary Authors*, and, for the younger reader, *Something About the Author*. These books, available in any library, synthesize interviews from many sources and usually include the literary genealogy that led to each writer's particular approach. Then read *those* books. And so on.

I also urge you to read randomly and outside what you want to write. I write literary fiction, but I have certainly profited from reading thrillers and science books and comics and Greek tragedies and magazine ads and fortune cookies.

What matters is that you are reading and *thinking* as you do. But how to do that? Here are some tips:

1. Recognize that there is no single right way to read as a writer, other than the general rule of reading closely.

2. Look behind the creation to understand the techniques of the

creator. That is, be the reader who gets wowed (or fails to get wowed) by the text and, simultaneously or in a reread, see how and why the author is eliciting certain reactions from you.

3. Understand that reading is a two-way street when you're a writer. The closer you read, the more tricks and techniques you can learn to use as a writer. *And* the more you write, the more you understand the way a writer's mind works, and so the more clearly you'll see others' tricks and techniques.

4. As you read a piece, notice your emotional reactions to and thoughts about the characters and story, and when those reactions shift in one direction or another. Perhaps you should even make notations in the margins (yes, with a pen; this is why it's good to purchase books) to remind you that here you laughed, here you got bored, here you felt an urgency to continue.

When you have finished the piece, step back and think about the larger, or macro, elements, such as overall story, pacing, character development, structure, consistency of voice. See if you think these were done well, given how you reacted emotionally and how they made you think. Then reread the piece, looking at the more minute, or micro, elements. These include how the voice was created, how the characters were introduced, what the metaphors refer to, how the transitions were accomplished, if the sentence variety was satisfying. When examining micro elements, you might want to break the text into smaller and smaller units—first the area between space breaks, then groups of paragraphs, then a single paragraph, then a sentence, then a clause, then a word. Study the function of *everything* (recognizing, of course, that the more you know about writing, the more you'll be able to see). If you look closely, you will come to understand why you thought and felt as you did during your initial reading.

5. Maintain these two important fundamental beliefs (assuming you are reading the text fairly and closely):

• The writer was in control when he wrote this piece. Everything you think and feel as you read it you are meant to think and feel. This includes every connotation, every whatever-happened-to-that-eccentric-minor-character question, every fleeting contemplation of the coincidence that the hero's hat is yellow and the villain hates sunlight—everything.

• Your reaction is never wrong. In other words, trust your doubts. If, for instance, you aren't feeling truly sad when the puppy gets hit by the motorcyclist—though it's clear that you're *supposed* to feel sad—trust that the text is awry, not you. Then try to see why the text didn't convince you to feel sorrow. If you look closely, you'll almost always come up with a good reason.

6. As you're reading, make a list of each element you want to examine, focusing on those you are most concerned about in your own writing. You might also want to explore elements you haven't yet used yourself, because the longer you are a writer, the more techniques you will want to know.

7. Recognize that the more you do of this, the better you'll get at it. Practice makes proficiency.

8. Feel free to scrutinize not only elements you've already been aware of but elements that you've never heard anyone talk about. I usually make up categories for things I haven't seen in a text before, and then get a whole new class of elements to look at in my own work. Let's say you're studying voice, and you realize the writer found a way to convey voice that you'd never noticed elsewhere. Make up a category ("shifts in typeface," maybe, or "unusual punctuation"). This will expand your own vision, because you'll see so many more possibilities.

9. Recognize that every writer you look at will differ from one piece to another. This is because each writer has different strengths, and each piece is unique.

10. Look at books and magazines not just to learn how to write but also to investigate the possibilities of publishing. Remember that every publication was the product of an author whose work matched the critical requirements and needs of an editor. Therefore, you can look at books and magazines as guides for what editors in general want, and for what this editor in particular wants. In books, this means paying attention to the different publishing houses, noting, for instance, that the kinds of styles and subjects published by Knopf differ from those published by Morrow or Pocket. In magazines, this means paying attention to all aspects of the magazine—the ads, the nonfiction articles, even the photographs—so you understand the audience the publication seems to be aiming for. Not only will you then learn craft from reading, but you will become much more astute about the writing business.

If you follow this basic procedure, you will quickly come to feel that every piece of printed material is a priceless teacher and, as a result, that there is no area of writing that you cannot teach yourself. Your best university is on your shelves.

WRITING CLASSES AND WRITING PROGRAMS

But let's say you want more guidance than books themselves will provide. You have heard about classes and graduate programs in writing, and you think they might offer you something you don't feel you can give yourself right now. What are you getting into?

Most writing classes, whether held at the local YMCA or part of the curriculum at an Ivy League college, are taught by what is called the workshop method. This means that when a student brings a piece of writing to class, everyone in the room reads and discusses it as a group, focusing both on strengths and weaknesses, so the writer gets opinions from everyone and perhaps even consensus.

The specific approach to the workshop varies from teacher to teacher. Some leave the students seated in rows while others have the students sit in a circle. Some ask the students to read the work in advance, maybe marking it up with a pen so the writer can receive detailed written responses. Others ask the writer to read the story aloud so class comments are more immediate. Some teachers ask students to speak one at a time, perhaps specifying (as I do with my students) that the initial comments be positive. Other teachers prefer students to critique in a free-for-all. Most teachers ask that the writer who is in the hot seat remain silent (and hence not defensive) until the end of the discussion, at which point questions, not excuses, are welcome.

Obviously, the workshop approach to teaching writing can be extremely difficult for the writer if the teacher does not provide the proper structure and tone for the class. A teacher who encourages mutual support and constructive criticism will conduct a class quite different in feeling from that of a teacher who sits back while the three most vocal students savage a writer and the other ten students cower self-protectively. It is no wonder, then, that one of the most important components of a successful writing class is the writing teacher.

Good writing teachers are orchestra conductor, Secretary of State, archeologist, sage, den mother, and lifeguard all rolled into one. To paraphrase Flannery O'Connor, good writing teachers can't implant the gift of writing in a student, but if they find a gift already there, they try to keep it from growing in a glaringly wrong direction. To accomplish this, good teachers foster an atmosphere in which students feel safe to write, speak, and listen, yet also feel compelled to question themselves, discover insights, and take risks. Good teachers are neither brutal nor coddling, controlling nor indifferent; they are no more tolerant of arrogance than of laziness, and no less cognizant of passion than of fear. They have warmth as well as high standards. A sense of humor. Enthusiasm. Flexibility. And offer *useful comments in every class.*

Sometimes students assume that, for a teacher to be good, she should have published a lot or at least published work that the student loves. This can be true, but it is a mistake to make this a requirement. My best writing teacher had published plays, which I wasn't interested in writing, but his approach was so generous and productive that my former classmates and I still speak glowingly about him. Conversely, one of my friends took a course from a world-famous novelist and found him to be bombastic, erratic, irrational, and vicious—exalting her story one week with profuse promises that she would bypass dues-paying and go directly to literary canonization, and then the next week, when rereading the *exact same story,* bellowing for thirty minutes about the deluded morons who dumb down his class.

You don't need a *Who's Who* laureate to learn. Sadists can be in print, angels can still be struggling. Books are no proof of goodness. Publications don't count as much as heart.

A good teacher can be as tricky to find as a good therapist. And, as with a good therapist, only the client—or student—can be the judge. So approach classes with your mental lights on. If you attend a few sessions of a class and feel the teacher embodies many of the qualities you don't respect in a person, then you can make an educated guess that you don't have a good teacher. If, however, you enter the class and find yourself stimulated by new understandings, inspired to keep writing, and plunging eagerly into work built on lessons learned in class, then you can safely conclude that you have struck teacherly gold.

Of course, few teachers are unconditionally rotten, and few are utterly spectacular. Like friends, most teachers fall somewhere between the poles, and one of your tasks as a student is to discern when your teachers are guiding you toward clarity, originality, and a sense of competence and faith, and when they are leading you closer to confusion, imitation, and a sense of ineptitude and doubt. The longer you take classes, the more easily you can make such assessments, but until then, try to use common sense and see what feels right for you. Also, recognize that it might take quite a while to see where your teacher falls on the rotten-spectacular continuum, and that you might be well into a semester before you realize what you've gotten yourself into. If you see the teacher is closer to spectacular, good for you. (For more on this, see "Mentors" later in this chapter.) If, though, you see the teacher is closer to rotten, you can still learn a lot, both by taking in the valuable instruction and by doing antilearning (learning the opposite of instruction that is counterproductive). You can learn from all teachers, even if you don't learn exactly what they want.

That said, how should you find these teachers? Should you take writing classes occasionally, one at a time, at the local Y or in continuing education programs? Or should you go whole hog into studying writing and sign up for a graduate degree?

This depends on many considerations. If you have a very busy life that you cannot set aside for a couple of years, and/or you are not yet sure how much of a commitment you are willing to make to writing, then individual writing classes will be better for you. You can find them in many high school and university continuing education evening programs. Call all the local schools in your area (look under "Schools & Colleges" in the yellow pages) and ask for their catalogs. Try Ys and arts centers as well. You might also find people like me who teach out of living rooms or at a table in a coffee shop; such nonaffiliated writers can be found through advertising in bookstores and local newspapers or by word of mouth. I have also been contacted by an especially resourceful student who simply read and enjoyed a work of mine in a magazine, sent me a letter in care of that publication, and asked me to teach her. When you want to learn, no door is necessarily closed to you.

Maybe, though, you have already taken some writing classes or have already done a huge amount of writing on your own. Now you want something more substantial, comprehensive, and focused. You have heard about writing programs, and you think that you might want to attend one. How do you go about finding the right one for you?

The best approach is also the easiest. An organization called

Associated Writing Programs, or AWP, publishes the *AWP Official Guide to Writing Programs*, which lists all the creative writing programs in the United States. Each of the more than three hundred programs is described in detail, with discussion of how much the students actually write versus how much they are required to take other, non-writing, courses. This book is your Geiger counter to writing programs. If you read it thoroughly, you stand a chance of finding a program that is suited to you. AWP's address is Associated Writing Programs, Tallwood House, Mail Stop 1E3, George Mason University, Fairfax, VA 22030. Their number is (703)993-4301.

But should you attend a program? After all, until sixty or so years ago, writers never studied writing in institutions; they learned by doing. What are the major reasons people give for going to a writing program, and is there any validity to those reasons?

1. You want guidance. Most writing teachers can give you this, provided they have experience and compassion and are secure enough not to be threatened by a student's eagerness or abilities. Almost all writing teachers offer technical guidance, some having more breadth or depth than others. Many teachers offer emotional guidance, and with luck and some degree of assertiveness, you can find one who will.

2. You want to make contacts in publishing. Occasionally writing programs expose students to agents and editors. The Iowa Writers Workshop is renowned for being a must-visit spot for many people in the business. But any top program (Columbia, Stanford, etc.) might attract editors and agents, even if it is just to attend some of the more prestigious readings that are inevitably held there.

Teachers in all programs may also connect you to their agent and/or offer advice on the magazines that might be best for you. Some might even give you editors' names.

3. You want to be in a community of writers. You will get this in a writing program. After all, it is a collection of people who are actively writing and, in the case of your teachers, actively publishing. But each student and teacher will view writing in his or her own way. Some students in my graduate program were there because they were committed to being authors. Others were there because they'd lost their jobs and didn't know what else to do. Some wanted to learn to write well. Some already wrote well and just wanted two years of unobstructed time in which to get a book together. Some teachers care

about language and not narrative; others narrative and not language. Some will always love your work because it is in first person or set in Toledo. Others will hate it for the same reasons. Some eschew the market; others insist you study it.

So, yes, you will be in a community of writers, but be prepared for it to be a diverse community. You will find people who agree with your tastes, needs, and goals and people who don't.

4. You want to climb out of your current career abyss and become a professional writer. Writing programs may assist you in becoming a much better writer, and in rare instances they can lead directly to writing contracts.

But bear in mind the comments in "Finding Money" in chapter four. Even with a degree in writing, you will have a tough time supporting yourself as a writer. This is sad but true.

5. You want to teach writing. In most cases, you need an M.A. or M.F.A. to teach writing. (Exceptions are made for older writers who began in the days before master's programs, and people with substantial publications who have achieved a high degree of success.) Hence, writing programs can be very helpful, because they allow you to obtain one of the most fundamental elements of a successful resume.

Okay, now you know what your main motivations for attending a writing program are likely to be. What can you expect? Here are some pros and cons.

Pros: Access to people who have been writing a lot longer than you and so have insights and expertise that you don't. Access to writers you have long admired and wish to know better. Access to university libraries and scholars who can help you supplement the knowledge you already have. Access to new writing friends whose opinions and strengths you will come to value and who might remain with you the rest of your life. Opportunities to explore the many ideas and experiences offered by a university environment. Opportunities to view the hardships and blessings of the lives of several professional writers. A few years of structured writing time, with regular deadlines, during which the marketplace is not the sole judge of quality. The social role of a student, which means more freedom than you might otherwise feel to explore unusual or iconoclastic thoughts.

Cons: If the school uses the workshop approach, and your teachers are not as strong and careful as they could be, you might come to fear writing anything that will elicit antagonistic or bitter comments from others, and consequently might write according to peer pressure rather than to your inner voice. Along the same lines, you might find yourself neglecting your inner voice because you are focusing excessively on external validation: class comments, teachers' smiles, final grades. Either way, you might be learning more about driving someone else's train than about jumping off their tracks and hopping on your own.

So should you go or not?

If you really feel you want to be around people who are interested in writing, and are hell-bent on getting something out of it—even if that's in the form of antilearning—then go. If you feel the cons outweigh the pros, or the lack of guarantees outweigh the definite assurances, then try to teach yourself instead. Just remember that, unlike having kids, the choice of whether or not to attend graduate school is reversible: If you hate being in school, you can leave, and if you stop wanting to teach yourself, you can go.

MENTORS

Whether or not you attend writing classes or programs, you might find yourself revering a single writer or teacher. Or else you might *want* to revere a single writer or teacher. Is this a good thing? What can you get out of it?

I have always had a bit of a bias when it comes to mentors, which is that they are wonderful assets to any writer's career—as long as the writer keeps in mind that no mentor can be helpful in all areas, and that it is important to grow away from the mentor at some point. In other words, intellectual/creative parenting is enormously beneficial, but all writers must eventually cease relying on the advice of mentors and come into their own, maturing until they can mentor themselves. Otherwise they will remain dependent, always needing approval before they can know if they have pulled off a story, always seeking advice before they can make any business decisions, and—the most damaging pitfall—always seeing their mentors' visions instead of their own.

Listen to your mentor, enjoy your mentor, learn from your mentor. But don't forget your inner voice. It can lead you to worlds where no other writer, including your mentor, has ever dreamt of going.

That said, beginning writers can find good mentors anywhere—in writing classes or programs, in correspondence with published authors, in the letters and diaries of deceased novelists. All that matters is that you trust your mentor enough to admit your needs, and then trust him enough to follow his counsel. Good mentors can also be collages of several people; perhaps from your teacher you get technical suggestions, from your correspondence you get publishing tips, and from the diaries of deceased novelists you get emotional support.

I mentioned earlier in this chapter that one of my students contacted me after reading a story of mine in a magazine. In fact, the purpose of Marisol's initial letter was to find a mentor. She wanted someone who could offer knowledge, experience, and wisdom, who could listen carefully to her concerns and respond constructively, and who, above all else, believed in her. I was so impressed at her cleverness at finding me and at her care in composing the letter that I called Marisol after receiving her letter. We spoke, she asked if she could hire me as a teacher, and over the months, as we got to know each other and I became even more impressed—this time by her work—we developed a bond that has proven helpful to us both. Marisol trusts my judgment and learns to write better; I have faith in her abilities and have the pleasure of watching her grow. Marisol gets inspiration and education; I get inspiration and gratification. We both know that my job will be done when she can incorporate my faith in her to such a degree that I cease being a regular need and turn instead into an occasional treat. Together we are working toward that goal while enjoying our relationship every step of the way.

Mentor-student relationships are about the richest ones available to beginning writers. I had several when I was struggling. One respected teacher applauded me for taking risks; another made me see the absurdity of modeling my structures on those of other writers; and most of the rest were dead, brilliant artists whose lives and writings provided models. Each one was a connection I treasure. Now when I write I always hear my own inner voice, but those earlier voices still babble at me from the sidelines, reminding me about the basics, the bottom lines, and what I have that's special.

DEALING WITH THE INFLUENCE
OF OTHER WRITERS

You can learn a great deal from other writers. But your education will be incomplete if you don't learn how to sort out your own thoughts from what other writers suggest.

This can happen whether the writer is your mentor, friend, or favorite author. When we respect other writers, we take what they say seriously, sometimes so seriously that it overrides anything *we* say. Our favorite novelist states in an interview that all writers should read science textbooks for a fundamental understanding of how the world works. We dutifully purchase a chemistry text, crack it open, and find ourselves in a torture chamber. But the novelist said to read it, so we try again. Our mind meanders to the fat content of the crackers on our desks, the boy with the buckteeth in eighth grade chemistry, Albert Einstein. We try to focus on the page. *Fe*—isn't that a Yiddish exclamation of exasperation? *Na*—isn't that the vernacular for "no"? We look at our arms and try to see chemical reactions on the skin. We yawn. Finally we put the book down and decide we are not an author.

Or we show a story to our closest writing friend. He tells us the ending is a major misfire and that if we want it to work, we have do thus and so. We try to do thus and so, but it comes out stiff, false. We dream up innovative ideas on what we could do to the original ending so that it would work, but James said to do thus and so, and since we can't, we put the story in a drawer, figuring that if we can't do it his way—*the* way—we must retreat entirely.

This happens time and again with writers. It's almost a formula: young writer who is a little less confident than he could be absorbs a declaration from another writer who seems considerably more confident. Young writer is wowed; the declaration is made with such assurance that it must be true. Young writer gloms onto that declaration, forsaking his own thoughts. Hence, young writer steps that much further away from himself, his inner voice, his own developing confidence.

When I was in college, I had a lean, goateed teacher in anthropology, Mr. M., who week after week repeated his two main rules of fieldwork. The first one was this: Listen to every single thing the natives say. The second one: Don't believe a word of it.

That is, take it all in, but always maintain enough sense of self that you are able to be skeptical when appropriate.

So how do you keep yourself from being swayed by others? How do you know when to listen to them and when to yourself?

I believe that the first order of business for all writers is to listen to themselves. This generally means that it's important to form your opinions about your own or someone else's story before you receive any input from others—before you show your story around and before you discuss someone else's work. By holding on longer to your privacy, you give yourself time to let your thoughts settle and to develop significant reasons for why you believe as you do. This way, when you encounter other opinions (in class, over the phone, in reviews), you can assess calmly and rationally whether you agree or disagree with them and remind yourself that your opinions count.

What if you don't have the time to form your opinions before you hear theirs? Most likely, this will occur when you are writing with an externally imposed deadline, such as the day when you are on the hot seat in your class or the day your manuscript must get to your editor. Whenever you find yourself dealing with the world before your opinions have gelled, remember that your thoughts are important. You might want to believe that everything a particular writer or teacher or editor says is "true," but you must remind yourself that you need time to come to your own conclusions. So hand the piece in on time, but keep rereading it on your own. And when others offer their opinions, remember your boundaries. (See chapter three.) Remember the opportunities you buy with continued patience. (Ditto.) Be willing to work more. And most importantly, don't devalue yourself.

I listened to everything the goateed Mr. M. said, not realizing that he would prove the veracity of his own two rules of fieldwork. Mr. M., it turned out, delighted in denigrating my other anthropology teachers because their academic concerns differed from his. For months I felt uneasy sitting in his room, listening to him snicker about my professors, watching his face glow like Rasputin beneath the buzzing fluorescent lights. At first I wondered if I should adopt his disdain for my other teachers; his put-downs were delivered with such assurance that it seemed he might in fact perceive these teachers better than I and so could detect frivolousness where I saw depth, gibberish where I saw knowledge. Gee, I wondered, quivering in my chair, maybe he was *right*. But finally one day my critical faculties came riding in like the cavalry over the hill; as I sat there in class, watching Mr. M.'s upper lip curl back for a new verbal catapult, I suddenly recognized that he was not "right" or able to perceive better than I. Mr. M. was merely a grouch with a need to squander his lecture time on shredding his colleagues. And from that moment on I listened to everything he said, but I never believed a word of it.

Just because someone has a big personality doesn't mean he is the Sultan of Truth. He may in fact be vehemently full of baloney.

You can learn a lot from listening. You can learn a lot more from listening critically.

DEFINING YOURSELF AS A WRITER

Throughout this book, I have talked a lot about saying no. This includes giving yourself permission, setting boundaries, and assessing priorities. But none of that will hold together if you don't work at developing a mental image of yourself as a writer.

This is not something that comes because you will it to be so, but because you make it happen through action. Your self-image as a writer can take root only after you have structured your time so you can write, and then, during your writing hours, *you write.* That is, the blueprint is drawn up, and now you're constructing the cathedral.

The new self-image won't occur in a single day. It will require time, probably several weeks or months, before you find that you are starting to see yourself differently. But then one morning you'll wake up and realize that, unlike before you started, you now truly accept the need for patience, and humility, and tenacity, and all the other big antidotes. Indeed, you have incorporated them into your being, every day a little more completely, and now have a sense of self as hard-working, hard-thinking, striving to improve, and amenable to waiting. And you will feel good about yourself, because you're doing what you want to do, and it's working.

However, when you first cross this monumental but invisible threshold from wanting to acting, other people will probably, for a while, keep defining you in the old ways. You are only the same old office secretary, or their same old brother, or just another lawyer with an interesting hobby. Not a Dickens—ha! You're just a Carol or a Russell, only now you're on this weird kick, like a grapefruit diet or weekend jogging. It's just a phase. You'll get back to your old self soon.

But if you have come to define yourself as a writer—and you are *writing*—you won't want to get back to your old self.

Others may have trouble with your persistence and may treat you just as they did before you committed yourself to your writing. An author of a five-book science fiction series plays basketball with buddies who still act as if he has never published at all. An M.F.A. student has problems with her co-workers; they invite her to lunch and she must decline, explaining that she writes on her lunch hour. What have you published? they then ask. Nothing?! Well, how quaint, the girl wants to write. One of my students gets a call every day from a friend who tells her, "Hurry up or give up." Another student has a husband who refuses to read her work, as though her writing won't exist if he doesn't pay attention. People sometimes have difficulty accepting this new definition of us.

When you have defined yourself as a writer and are living out that definition by actually writing, you'll know what to do with such behavior. You'll remember "No." You'll seek support elsewhere. You'll realize that such seemingly prying questions as "What's it about?" and "Aren't you published yet?" are meant to show interest, not nosiness, and that the speakers are probably romanticizing the writing process, unaware of the mental privacy and length of time it requires. They want to know if you are the mythological rising literary star they read about in magazines. Of course, literary stars are writers primarily and stars only secondarily. The same applies to you. With this realization, you will be able to respond politely but firmly to their questions—"I'm sorry, I don't talk about works in progress," and "Writing takes a long time; I'll tell you when I'm published." Some people can't let themselves see that you *could* be a literary star—and consequently moving in a direction away from them—which would explain why they might refuse to look at your work. And this will make you feel sorry for them. Because at this point you will be focusing on your writing rather than on how others wish to see you.

You don't have to give detailed answers. Let others keep thinking of you as someone who can't, or won't, or (*My god what's wrong with her!*) hasn't yet. You have your inner voice, which is more than most people ever get. With it, you can be strong and not let yourself get batted about by anyone. Eventually, because you give them no choice, they'll come around and see you as you have long since been seeing and enjoying yourself.

CHAPTER SIX

BEFORE THE DRAFT

It's an old truism about writing: All you need is a pen and paper. But everyone who has ever tried to write knows that you need more, much of which must develop before you even begin writing. What are the best ways to get yourself ready to write?

THE RIGHT MINDSET

People who haven't written at all often corner me at weddings and dinner parties and tell me how much they want to write. "I have a great novel inside me," they say, and then proceed to explain this phantom book, telling me about the narrative and characters, and how it's going to be a great book, a best-seller. "So write it," I tell them, which precipitates not a considered mulling over of the time and commitment involved, but more boasting: the setting, the title, the final scene. The world will think they're brilliant! People will purchase ten copies each—no one will ever want to buy any other book! By the time I manage to escape, I know the entire content, and I have learned all the reasons why they will win a MacArthur Genius Fellowship, but I also know without a doubt that they are not going to write this or probably any other novel.

The best mindset for writing does not involve planning content or exulting over the great success-to-be. In fact, I've found that the students who had most thoroughly thought through their specific content and the students who had dwelled most obsessively on their future fame were the students least likely to do any real writing. They got so caught up in picturing what the book *should* be that they were unable to let it be what it *could* be. They got so caught up in seeing the flashbulbs at their penthouse publishing party that they couldn't climb the long staircase up from the breakfast table to the desk. They got scared. Few wrote, and those who did tended to convince themselves that they weren't good enough to reach their preestablished image, whether of the book itself or of their own glory, so they stopped. Then they either claimed they didn't want to write anyway (they have too much to do, etc.), or else they moaned, "What's wrong? I *know* what the book is about! I *know* I'm a great writer! Why can't I write?"

Their problem is rarely a lack of talent, and it might not even be the inability to say no. Their problem is that they haven't adopted the most effective mindset, which is this, in a nutshell: It's okay to think some about the starting point and the destination, but your focus needs to be on the journey.

I know you've heard this before, both in terms of writing and in terms of life (dating, college, spiritual enlightenment). You might be willing to accept it as a general concept, though if you're like most people, you don't really understand how to convert the concept into action. Sure, you get it as far as daily writing schedules and all that, but you're not clear on what's involved in your thinking itself, that is, in the components that make up this mindset. Over the years, I have tried to come up with a way to explain what's involved, and, after watching myself and others slip and slide our way through writing, I have identified three main components of the effective mindset:

1. Faith. You believe that you can and will persist, day after day, and that your work will lead to a valuable piece of writing.

2. Spirit of Adventure. You are delighted by the prospect of exploration. You know that every turn, whether planned or unplanned, will lead to new vistas and that some, though not all, will be just right.

3. Acceptance of the Process as a Process. You embrace the slow climb, knowing that with patience and multiple drafts you will work your way to something wonderful.

When combined, these three components provide writers with enough weatherproofing to head out and keep going, whether that's just to the end of the driveway or on a cross-country excursion, and to do so while remaining composed. This is what these "failed" students need—much more than they need to know, before they've written the first word, how chapter seventeen will end, or what they'll wear to the ceremony for the National Book Award.

Nothing has made this clearer to me than the story of Colleen, one of the most talented and difficult students I've ever had. Colleen's difficulty was not uncooperativeness or a poverty of desire but a persistently negative mindset. She believed she couldn't. She wanted to write a great epic of Irish history, covering generations of ill-fated romantic couplings and political scheming. She knew the opening. She knew the ending. She'd obsessed over this book for years, yet she couldn't get anywhere—including up to her study to try.

We spent most of our classes discussing her resistance to writing a book she claimed she wanted to write. At first, it seemed the problem was content-oriented; although she had moved to America years before, she feared alienating the family that remained in Ireland, knowing that they would recognize themselves in some of her details. Soon, though, we came to see that her resistance transcended this book and crippled other writing projects as well: On all new stories, Colleen would shoot out of the starting gate with gusto, write several pages of engrossing prose, and then stop. She knew what to say. But she couldn't do it.

In time we learned that a large part of the problem was her mindset. She had never finished a story, and so she believed she couldn't. In fact, she saw herself as a foreordained failure. It was as if she'd been branded at thirteen, when her writing had been ridiculed in class by a nun, and now she would never be able to shake off that mark. Furthermore, Colleen believed that she had to write the stories as she'd originally conceived them, without allowing herself to try new possibilities if the first ones didn't feel right along the way. And on top of all this, she was certain that if it didn't come out luminously from the get-go, then it was rubbish. Which of course meant that nothing was ever worth finishing. Which, in the case of her novel, meant that it wasn't even worth starting.

Colleen and I worked on changing this mindset by using the principles of cognitive therapy. Cognitive therapy is so important that it deserves its own section in this book.

COGNITIVE THERAPY

The premise of cognitive therapy is twofold. First, it's that we all walk around with a truckload of negative tapes that play and play in our heads, telling us we're no good, we're stupid, nothing we ever do will work, etc. Second, it's that these thoughts are irrational distortions; if we can recognize this, we can speak back to those tapes—in a sense, we erase the negative phrases by replacing them with positive ones. By doing this *consciously, and maybe even methodically*, we can change how we feel about life.

Cognitive therapy is a form of treatment usually given to people deeply mired in depression. I have seen it perform miracles on some friends; they turned their intransigent pessimism into enduring optimism, and so learned to smile, and gave themselves permission to try.

When it comes to writing, cognitive therapy can be used to alter a person's initial mindset. This is what I did with Colleen.

We began by having her keep a process journal a few minutes a day. (I explain process journals later in this chapter in "Warming Up.") In her process journal, Colleen recorded all her thoughts about the writing process as it pertained to herself. Over a few weeks, she came to see how frequently she sabotaged her writing by believing in her own worthlessness. "Rachel gave me a great assignment, but then this morning I was too lazy to get to it. I'm such a jerk." "I loved class last night yet I can't implement any of the lessons because I just know I'll never get any better." "Rachel read that last assignment and said it was very good, but then added that it needed revision. Writing is never going to work out for me."

We then wrote down all the negative statements and discussed them. Was she too lazy to write, and did laziness make her a jerk? No. Laziness, as we know from chapter two, is absurd expectations courted by fear. Maybe it is a trait we associate with jerks, but it does not make us into a jerk. And just because she didn't write this morning does not mean she can't write at all. It only means that if she believes it. The same goes with Colleen's believing she'll never get any better. Just because she's had trouble incorporating the lessons into her daily writing does not mean she'll never get any better. Maybe they weren't the right lessons for her right now, and even if they were, betterness takes time. Besides, Rachel also praised Colleen's draft, but Colleen couldn't hear that. Her final statement, that writing is never going to work out for her, is derived from equating the need for work with a self-perception of failure. Work only means work. It is not an acknowledgment of inadequacy.

Thus, by specifying the negative thoughts that had marooned her, we were able to dislodge them. We examined all the overgeneralizations (I didn't finish this story, so I'll never finish any story), the absolutes (I'll never, I'm always), the labeling (I'm a loser, I'm a bum), the black-and-whites (She just has talent and I don't, that's all there is to it), the dismissal of the positive (So what if my story is wonderful. It's not perfect and that's what counts). Then we addressed each logically and in writing and saw how fatuous every one of them was.

After this, we practiced. Every time Colleen tried to write and heard these negative tapes, she responded to them. So instead of taunting herself, she defended herself. Soon, she began to believe her defense. That is, she taught herself to alter her mindset—to move from a place of lack of faith to a place of faith, from a spirit of defeat to a spirit of adventure, from the belief that she had to be right immediately (and that "right" must fit her preconceptions of the book) to the acceptance that the writing process might just be, well, a process. And as soon as she began to do all this, she was able to begin and, at long last, stick with a new and excellent novel.

How to alter *your* mindset? I urge students to use a process journal and then follow this procedure. I also suggest they read a few books on cognitive therapy. (One of the most popular and readily available ones is *Feeling Good: The New Mood Therapy*, by David D. Burns, M.D., Avon Books, 1992.) But I add that none of these efforts will mean anything if the students aren't also actively *doing*, since the development of a positive mindset needs some time.

Ohhh, they sigh, shaking their heads. This will take forever.

Not so. Faith, the first component of the right mindset, can come fairly quickly. All you need is to be writing regularly, which will enable you to see that, if you keep at it, your words can't help but shape themselves into *something*, maybe even a full and remarkable story. Witnessing this act of creation will lead to your believing in yourself. Soon thereafter will come the spirit of adventure, the second component. This develops when you dare to experiment and find that— hey!—the braver you are, the better the writing seems to be. Once you have this evidence before your eyes, a spirit of adventure will evolve rapidly inside you. The third component of the right mindset, acceptance of the process as a process, tends to take the longest to develop. Beginning writers are usually resistant to revising, and when they finally step into those unknown waters, they are seldom comfortable enough with revision to attempt more than dainty, cosmetic changes (which, they find, do little to help their ailing stories). But at last the day arrives when, often out of desperation, they accept the comprehensive nature of revision. Then they revise not just the cosmetic things but everything—and then they revise again, and again. The text becomes fluid; process becomes how they see the world. This usually strikes as an epiphany of reassurance, a giant *So what's the big hurry?* Process is the promise of a payoff, and as a result it makes all future writing feel easier. (For more on revision, see "When Stuck in Later Drafts" in chapter eight.)

So work on those negative tapes until you develop all three components of the positive mindset. Then it will become much less likely that you will suffer through all the old fears before you sit down to write. Instead, you will probably sit down eagerly and serenely and almost always find that you get your writing done.

DEVISING SUPERSTITIONS

I used to write only with a special pen. It was inscribed with my name and skated across the paper with incomparable grace, and because I'd gotten it when I was an exchange student in England, it seemed enchanted, an Excalibur of silver and smoothness and ink. Although I took class notes in pencil, I did my *real* writing—my fiction and correspondence—only with my beloved pen and only in the most sacred spot: on my bed in my dormitory, where I would listen to loud Led Zeppelin through headphones with my window propped open, the earthy fragrance of the cornfield out back wafting pleasantly past my posters and rocking chair, past my books and lamp, all the way up to the top of my quilt.

Then one day I happened to set the pen on my windowsill when friends stopped by. We did our usual three hours of advice seeking and giving, and after they left, I turned back to the windowsill to retrieve my pen. It was gone. In a panic, I fled downstairs and bolted into the cornfield. But no matter how frantically I scrabbled among the cornstalks and poked through the shadows, I couldn't find that pen. It had sailed out of my life, and now it was no more.

Although it was only a small object, the loss felt like a death. I had relied on that pen to get me going, to make my images take shape, to draw all my narrative threads into one compelling conclusion. I had seen it as a magic wand. Now I had lost my magic.

For a few weeks I didn't write at all. I couldn't. Other ballpoints felt dry as an undipped quill, or else they leaked. Nothing would do. I would never recover.

But eventually someone loaned me a new pen. Not identical to the original, but a sleek gold pen made by a different company. I liked the way it felt in my hands; I set it on some paper, and lo! I could write with it. Shortly thereafter, I found that if I sat down at my typewriter and simply decided to write, I could do that as well. Then I found that I could write in places besides my bed and listen to sounds other than Led Zeppelin. The park near my house, for instance, or the rock garden behind the library. Trains. Diners. The writing was inside me, I saw; it was not the consequence of an ink-filled catalyst. This became even clearer the following year, when I got my hands on a new pen just like my old favorite. I clicked it on, pressed the ballpoint to the page, and found that, instead of skating, it felt heavy, slow, as if weighted. What had seemed perfect no longer seemed perfect. I had found I could be versatile, and that all the catalysts were inside me.

I have had friends who believed they could write only when they were naked, or sitting in their grandfather's easy chair, or riding an airplane over the Atlantic at sunset. Willa Cather felt she could begin writing only after reading the Bible. Truman Capote believed he couldn't write on anything but yellow paper, but that he also couldn't write if there were yellow roses in the room. Gail Godwin writes in her essay "Rituals and Readiness" that Toni Morrison feels her work will be weak unless she rises before the first colors of dawn, lights a candle, and walks about her house. Gail Godwin adds that she starts her own writing sessions by burning two sticks of incense, one handmade by a Tibetan monk, the other manufactured in Tokyo.

Writing superstitions can involve anything: time of day, location, presence of others, attire, objects. Their rate of success with us is not, of course, the consequence of the superstition itself (I've broken mirrors and had no years of bad luck; I've avoided a black cat in the morning and still had a horrendous day). Their success is the consequence of our belief. I don't believe in the connection between mirrors and luck, so that particular superstition doesn't matter to me. But I do believe—at the moment—in the connection between my writing and the doohickeys adorning my computer: I believe that I write much better when the back of my computer is dotted with pieces of polished quartz and my collection of plastic *Wizard of Oz* figurines. And because I believe this, and because the Wicked Witch still grins greenly at me from her perch and hasn't yet become litter in a cornfield, I probably *do* write better. Superstition is all belief— belief and availability.

Superstitions can be both useful and detrimental. If you believe you can write only on unlined paper, and you find that this does indeed work for you, go ahead and write on unlined paper. The superstition may well work to your advantage. If, however, you find yourself with the urge to write and you don't have any unlined paper in the house, you need to work on shelving the superstition for that time. Or if, after a few years, unlined paper ceases to perform its helpful function, then, again, deep-six the superstition. In either case, pick up other kinds of paper and try them out. Be enterprising—if you hate staying within the lines and all you can find is lined paper, then try turning the pad sideways, so your writing runs across the lines rather than within them. By being inventive and experimenting with one kind of substitute and then another, you will most likely hit on something that will work just as well for you or perhaps even better.

There is nothing wrong with superstitions, provided you don't become a slave to them, and you remain willing to explore new possibilities. Again, use a process journal to see what you like and believe and whether or not it actually works. Then you can keep track of your preferences, and know when to hold on to each superstition, and when it's appropriate to discard it and jump ship.

MAKING TIME

I have discussed this in several other areas of this book. (See "Finding Time to Write" and "Balancing Writing and Extra-Writing Activities" in chapter four, and "Defining Yourself as a Writer" in chapter five.) Those sections address wanting to write badly enough to plan ahead, prioritizing all writerly activities so writing itself comes out on top, getting a handle on other obligations by setting boundaries, and developing your self-image by enjoying all the benefits of writing.

Basically, here's the drill:

Think ahead.

Plan a schedule.

Keep your eye on your passion.

Say no.

And remember mortality. If you want to write, write, since there may be no next year. Before I begin a piece, I feel I must do it now, because if I don't and something happens to me, that story will never be born into the world. For the same reason, I keep going once I have gotten into the thick of a piece.

You *can* make the time. It's up to you.

WARMING UP

At last!

The time is arranged, the lucky footstool is beneath your feet, and you are feeling optimistic, adventurous, and ready to trust the process. So you settle in.

Now what?

I always recommend to my students that they start their writing time with a period of warming up. Warming up helps the many writing muscles get ready for more strenuous exercising. It eases you into the writing trance, slows your inner pace to the pace of your storytelling imagination, reminds your hand what it feels like to be a pitcher of words. That is, warming up gets you ready for the real work ahead.

Experiment to find the warm-up activity that is best for you. Your goal is to find the activity that most effectively submerges you into the dream state, so that when you finish your warm-up, you are able to slip right into writing. You might want to try one or more of the following options or explore others of your own.

Journal Writing. Journals can be used in numerous ways. There's the old standard of a meticulous log describing our day-to-day lives, in which we use complete, grammatically correct sentences, introduce all new characters, strive for the best word, and fancy that someone someday will reread these immortal statements. Then there's the emotional splat sheet, on which we dump all our fears and ecstacies without benefit of narrative and with a proliferation of fragments, exclamation points, and misspellings. And of course there is the inspiration closet, in which we record all our captivating story ideas and sparkling metaphors and every bon mot we've come across in our travels, sometimes even taping scissored articles into the pages.

However you approach a journal, you may find journal writing to be a helpful opening to your writing session. At its best, journal writing can slip you directly into a writing mode, separate you from your physical being, and nudge you away from experiencing while it propels you toward expressing.

For me, the best approach to a journal is to have no set rules except to date the entry. That way, there is no pressure to edit or invent some pithy phrase. I can strip away the verbal and emotional censors that, while useful in the world (great barriers to committing a social faux pas), hinder me on the page (great barriers to writing anything daring). Years ago I made a pact with myself that I would never show my journal entries to others or reread them myself. This has enabled me to write anything I want, without concern of being judged by anyone, including me. Thus I can loosen up through my journal writing, allowing me to be open and undaunted by the time I get to my work.

If you try journal writing as a warm-up, spend at least ten to twenty minutes on it at the beginning of your writing session.

Process Journal. This is a specific kind of journal, which I've referred to earlier in this chapter ("Cognitive Therapy"), and which I urge all beginning writers to have. Kept in a separate book from your regular journal yet just as private as a regular journal, a process journal is a record of your thoughts about the writing process, particularly as that process applies to you. For one or two minutes every day, you note one or two ideas you've had about writing, anything from how you wrote today at the bus stop versus yesterday in your living room, to how using a fountain pen over a ballpoint makes you feel more like a real author, to a quotation from Oscar Wilde about the process of revision and what you think about it, to your negative— and positive—tapes about yourself.

A process journal will familiarize you with the concept of process. It will also help you see what works best for you by giving you an outlet in which to register your many reactions to everything you try.

Letters/E-mail. Correspondence is a different kind of warm-up from journal keeping in that it is meant to be seen. Indeed, it is meant to be seen by a specific audience—the recipient. This may make the writing a bit more inhibited than it would be in a journal, but in return for that sacrifice you get some kind of direction. That is, some correspondents are interested in quantum mechanics and appreciate a subdued voice that relies on Latinate words, while others are more interested in your latest bomb of a date and appreciate a colloquial voice that relies on creative profanity. Some want description, maybe of your recent vacation with your family, the tasks you perform on the job; others prefer analysis, maybe what you think about your family's neuroses and your CEO's motivations and how your issues of dependence and authority are developing. Some write two-sentence letters; others go on for pages.

Letter writing necessitates that you consider the content, style, approach, and length that would be appreciated by your audience. Thus, by forcing you to write within some guidelines, letter writing might turn out to be more liberating than journal writing, where you have so many options you might not be able to write anything.

Since I was eight years old, I have corresponded with scores of people, ranging from close friends who moved out of state to relatives I've never met to acquaintances I shared an office with for one day. I believe that the years I spent writing to these pen pals were excellent training for learning about the subtleties of audience receptivity and the range of voices I could adapt. This training has helped me enormously in all my fiction, enabling me to have a kind of ventriloquism in my work. I could attribute this to my range of reading, but at least as important was my constant involvement with letter writing.

If you choose letter writing for your warm-up, write for at least twenty minutes. You need not complete the letter for the warm-up to be effective.

Freewriting. Freewriting works similarly to journal writing, and provides similar benefits. To freewrite, decide on a certain period of time (generally ten to twenty minutes). Then pull out a watch to time yourself and start writing anything. Stories. Free association. Grumblings. Babble. You are to write for the entire allotted period without cessation, even if you have no ideas. During the dry moments, simply write, "I don't know what to say, I don't know what to say," until an idea comes to mind. Then follow it wherever it goes. Write until the time period ends.

If you can relax, freewriting will loosen you up as few other activities can. You will find yourself pursuing topics and associations you had never thought about before. Perhaps you will even plunge into writing whole stories that you had no sense were inside you. Shortly before my collection of short stories went through its final edits, my editor asked me to come up with a new piece. Just in case we toss out one of the others, she said. I could see the logic, yet this assignment gnawed at me for weeks; I was too preoccupied with other aspects of my life to have even the speck of an idea. Finally I went to a library, determined to make some progress with this task. I sat down, pulled out paper, and decided that, since I had no ideas, I would just free-write. Twenty minutes, I figured, that's what I'd go for, and if I didn't come up with a story idea during that time, then I would simply freewrite another twenty minutes, and then another, until I hit on something useful. So I freewrote, chattering away until, near the end of the first twenty minutes, I hit on the idea of a teenager who pretends she's pregnant to con her folks into letting her stay home from school. I kept freewriting beyond the twenty minutes and found that, as she was playing this legitimate hooky in her house, an escaped convict broke into the back door and confronted her. Bingo—I had my premise: little congirl meets big convict. I freewrote for another three hours, and at the end I had the first draft of my story.

Freewriting can get you going, and it can keep you going. It can take you across new time zones in your unconscious, convey you over the curve of a globe you'd always been sure was flat. It can trade your old thinking for new, your skepticism for serendipity. And it can be more fun than you ever thought writing could be.

If you freewrite for your warm-up, start with ten minutes, though consider doing more; some of my students do forty-five minutes and so through freewriting alone complete most of that day's writing session.

CHAPTER SEVEN

DURING THE DRAFT

If writing were a spectator sport, as the comic group Monty Python once imagined when they placed a scribbling Thomas Hardy before cheering fans in a stadium, it would appear to the observer that nothing more is involved than the writer making marks on a paper or a computer screen as he transcribes a story from his mind to the page. To writers, however, it is plain that infinitely more is involved, almost all of which falls under the category of wrestling with your soul.

Writing is much more than the recording of words. It is much more than the unfolding of a story. Writing is a slow learning, through content, style, process, and daily evidence of your tenacity, of who you are, what you value, and what you want from life. Fight too hard as you write—be too resistant, prideful, frightened, defensive—and you are virtually guaranteed to quit. But give yourself over to writing— surrender your resistance, pride, fear, self-protectiveness—and you stand a chance of continuing. Plus, you will have drenched yourself in self-awareness, and that is a benefit few other disciplines can bestow as thoroughly as writing.

This may all sound very interesting but seem hard to apply to your particular situation. That's the purpose of this chapter. You probably think that if you are having trouble doing your writing, your problem is unique. It is true that your soul is unique, and hence so is the specific pattern and pace of your wrestling. But in all my years of writing and teaching, I have found that all of us writers are bedeviled by the same impediments; they just manifest themselves in different ways for each person. By understanding the universality of our difficulties, we can keep moving forward. If, however, we think that our difficulties are our cross—and only ours—to bear, then we will most likely stop.

These universal difficulties fall into the following categories: misreading (or not hearing) the inner voice, withholding personal investment when choosing material, fearing faith, resenting criticism, getting ensnared in delusions, and becoming paralyzed by aloneness.

In this chapter I discuss the above phenomena and pose suggestions for how to work through each with minimal fuss and maximal alacrity. By the end of the chapter, you should have a much better sense of how to wrestle with your soul so that you don't get discouraged and defeated, so that you can manage to keep writing that draft.

HEARING YOUR INNER VOICE

In chapter three, I defined the inner voice as "the internal aesthetic trail guide that directs us toward the great." The inner voice is each writer's unique intuition, which can, if listened to attentively, tell a writer how a piece is doing and whether it's done. In effect, the inner voice is a writer's Jiminy Cricket, a little squeaky conscience that says, "Trim that paragraph! Beef up that description! Make that ending more subtle!"

But the inner voice has two disadvantages that affect different stages of the writing process: The first disadvantage is that, during a first draft, a writer may mistakenly interpret fear as his inner voice; and the second, that in later drafts the inner voice is, at least initially, rather shy, and if a writer isn't careful, he might ignore it.

Let's go through these one at a time.

The Inner Voice and the First Draft. During the first draft, you may think you hear your inner voice insisting that you are screwing up. Your inner voice is howling—right as the words are emerging from your hands—that the metaphor comparing the orchid to female sexuality is hackneyed, or that the captain of the ship needs a description better than "grizzled." Or that you need to change the setting from the porch to the backyard. Or, perhaps, it is bellowing something less technical, something more along the lines of, "This is trash, you illiterate dilettante. Hang it up now."

If that happens (it probably will), you need to remember two points. The first is that, in your first draft, you don't need to fret about the details. Stop only when you have hit a *major* snag. Otherwise, keep going until you have completed the draft. After all, it is more important to get out a remarkably imperfect first draft than to stall halfway through a brilliant one. Imperfection can always be addressed in later drafts, but a brilliant half-draft is no draft at all.

The second point to remember is that *fear is not the same as the inner voice.* You may find yourself duped into fusing the two, but after many first drafts of many stories, you'll begin to see the distinction: Fear screams, while the inner voice whispers. Fear throws manipulative, negative-thought temper tantrums, while the inner voice prods gently. Fear seems thunderous, paralyzing. It demands we stop. It wants to shackle our hands, rip us out of the process, make us prove to ourselves that we are no good at writing and, consequently, at anything. The inner voice says to go on but throws in qualifiers. *Later on you need to remember that the orchid metaphor is off,* it murmurs in our ear. *Don't forget you've rushed the description of the ship captain; you'll want to expand that in the next draft.* The inner voice is patient. It knows it will keep nagging until you act, and so it lets you go on until you act. Fear, however, is an avalanche of prohibitions. *You can't use that idiom, you idiot! That fight scene's a loser, you moron!* Fear castigates and insults and insists on immediate response. The inner voice cajoles and suggests and waits until you get around to paying attention.

So, during a first draft, just keep pressing ahead. Don't stop. When fears try to thwart you, work on cognitive therapy techniques until you can keep going. (Described in chapter six, these techniques involve identifying your negative thoughts, recognizing them as illogical, and countering them with logical, positive thoughts.) When your inner voice tries to correct you, jot down what it says in your margins or in another location and keep going.

End every writing session with a stint in your journal so that you can give your inner voice a place to express its concerns. That way it's all recorded. You'll be able to knock off for the day with the knowledge that you've given your inner voice the respectful airing it deserves and with the assurance that you will have those thoughts in ready-to-use form the next time you sit down to write.

The Inner Voice and Later Drafts. But when you move into your revision drafts, you need to recognize the other characteristic of the inner voice: shyness. Actually, this isn't shyness as much as a learned response; your inner voice is so accustomed to being ignored that it has trained itself to speak faintly, or maybe even scaled itself down from an articulate voice to mumbled misgivings.

My student David is currently struggling with this problem. He recently handed me a story, grinning with pride, saying, "I've revised it, and it's done." I read it for class and saw that it wasn't done; it still needed to be tightened in the beginning, paced more slowly in the middle, made less preachy at the ending. When we met in class and I went through all this, I thought he might be surprised at my comments, but instead he responded, "Gee, I'd thought the same things, but I didn't make the changes." "Why not?" I asked. He paused, then shrugged. "I didn't trust that my perceptions were right. They just hadn't seemed that important." His inner voice *had* been speaking to him—a major step for any writer. Unfortunately, it wasn't yet speaking loudly and assertively enough for him to respect. Sometimes he even convinced himself that it was not speaking at all.

How can you persuade your inner voice to speak up and be heard?

The primary means to hearing your inner voice more clearly is to read your later drafts out loud, over and over and over. If you change one word, read the whole piece out loud again.

Reading aloud separates your writing voice from your inner voice. When you read out loud, you are reading your writing voice, while your inner voice remains inside your mind. Thus, you allow room for a dialogue between the two. That is, you read a sentence aloud. The inner voice squeaks that it's not quite right, so, if you're paying attention, you stop and work on the sentence. Then you read the sentence aloud again and see how the inner voice likes it this time. Do this repeatedly—a hundred or more times if necessary. The inner voice needs to be coaxed from its whisper, and just one or two or five read-throughs will not achieve that goal. The inner voice is like a child: It needs a safe place so that it can speak. That safety will come only when you prove by returning to work on and read the story again and again that you will be there, listening.

The more you read aloud, the more explicitly your inner voice will speak to you. Then you'll know the difference between the inner voice and fear, and the inner voice and silence, and you'll be that much closer to feeling confident and self-reliant with your work and, by extension, with yourself.

CHOOSING YOUR MATERIAL

When people ask what I write about, I summarize my basic concepts and narratives, but no matter what my phrasing or which book I'm discussing, their next comment is almost always either "Where do you get your ideas?" or "Well, do I have a story for you!" The first question assumes that ideas come from research or the imagination; the second, that ideas come from real-life incidents.

The truth is that ideas come from all those places. What matters is not where they originate, but what the ideas do inside you.

When writers speak about their "material," they are referring both to the content of the story—the "idea" behind it—and to the themes of the story—what the story is saying about humanity and the laws of the universe. For instance, many writers write about sexuality, but some do so in a way that says people are cold and deserving of empty marriages; others in a way that says people are romantic and justice will prevail in love; others portray people using sexuality to connect, and suggest that is good; others present people using sexuality to control, and suggest *that* is good.

Same overall content, different approaches. In other words, different material.

How do you find *your* material?

This is one of the biggest quandaries for beginning writers and for advanced writers who have taken time away from their work. Either nothing seems worthy of their writing energies, or everything does. They can't muster the desire, or else they can't discriminate between desires. So they are left at a loss, floundering, getting nowhere, not continuing.

But choosing your material isn't that mysterious or troublesome an endeavor. It comes in a very simple way: by being observant of the world *and at the same time* reflective of yourself. Or, to put it another way, by being externally alert while being introspectively perceptive.

In practice, this means a two-stage process. First, keep your eyes and ears open to all that exists outside you: a melancholic song on the radio, refrigerators dumped in the wetlands outside town, an overheard conversation at the service station, an albino cat darting across a busy road, your dry cleaner's fleeting references to her Navaho lover, a nightmare about your ex-husband getting engaged to your daughter, a friend's anecdote about her mother's escape from

Germany. Look at it all. By "all" I mean everything from such sources as these:

- Newspapers, radio, and television—News, ads, songs, comics, op ed pieces, offhand remarks, etc.
- Conversation, both direct and overheard
- Experiences, both recent and so old as to be mythological
- Dreams and slivers of dreams (those foggy semiconscious images at the beginning and end of sleep)
- Photographs, paintings, greeting cards
- Books
- Objects, scents, sounds
- Combinations of all the above

Some of what you are seeing will do nothing for you. But some of it will fascinate you, set all your neurons on alert, throw your inquisitiveness into fifth gear, catch your heart and won't let go. This stuff of fascination will lead to your content.

Then begin the second stage of the process: Think about *why* this particular object/conversation/etc. captivated you. You need not think about this overtly, and certainly you need not do so before you actually begin to write. But when you have begun writing and are developing characters, you need to probe inside yourself for where the emotions and concerns of that object/conversation/etc. intersect with the emotions and concerns of your own life. *Do not write what you know. Instead, write what matters to you.*

Your material is content in which you feel a substantial personal investment, but it need not be drawn entirely from your autobiography. As John Gardner says of the "Write what you know" dictum, nothing is more limiting to the imagination, and nothing will more rapidly activate our self-censoring mechanisms. Writing is not meant to hook us into tighter and tighter orbits around ourselves. Writing is meant to get us to expand and explore and examine, to tinker with our concept of gravity, to question whether day should be night. That's not just so we learn. That's also where the fun comes in.

One of my most successful stories was about a loving elderly couple who try to share each other's dreams. I was in my twenties when I wrote this, so I did not *know* about the elderly the way I knew about all the ages I had already lived. But I did know about love and dreaming and realized as I wrote that what mattered to me and my characters was that we both wanted our romantic relationships to last—although, since my characters were elderly, they needed to face the likelihood of their relationship ending due to death. My emotions and concerns were not identical to theirs, but my emotions and concerns overlapped with theirs. Therefore, I could write the story feeling very connected to them.

Content is not what really matters in writing. Emotions and concerns are the key.

How to know your own emotions and concerns?

- Keep a journal
- Bring deep talks with friends to definite, I've-really-learned-something conclusions rather than amorphous, superficial, drift-off endings
- Consider seeing a counselor—therapist, clergyperson, hypnotist
- Engage in reverie-producing activities, such as physical exercise, repetitive household chores, gardening
- Be honest with yourself
- Eschew self-evasion and denial
- Think

The key to finding your material is to feel so compelled by an idea that you want to learn why and how it matters to you. Then you can shack up with that material for a while. When you feel the urge to move on, you'll be equipped to begin a new search, because then you'll have a deeper understanding both of how the search is done and of the identity of the person who is searching.

MAINTAINING FAITH

I have addressed faith in other sections of this book, especially the sections on "Confidence" in chapter two, "Humility" in chapter three, and "The Right Mindset" in chapter six.

Aside from those comments, the main point to bear in mind about faith is that it walks hand-in-hand with patience. Patience generates faith; faith generates patience. When you give yourself time, you see that you *can* do it. Hurrying obfuscates faith. "I can't!" you wail, as you despair over ever getting to the next stage in your writing. But with patience, you recognize that you *can*. Slowly. One day at a time, maybe moving pebbles instead of boulders. But you will get there, even a there you are currently unable to see.

HANDLING CRITICISM

You finish the story (or at least you think so). You decide to spring it on the world and see how others react. Even if the story is not about your life, you probably feel coupled to it, that it reflects on *you*. So if your friend reads a story you've written and hands it back, saying, "Well, the ending is a little pat," you think, "My God! She thinks it rots! She thinks I'm a buffoon! She doesn't like me!" Or else you might respond to criticism with anger and defensiveness. Once I was asked to critique a story that an acquaintance had written. I dutifully made comments with my red pen and gave it back her. This woman became furious, her rage taking on Ghaddafi-esque proportions. She called my answering machine at home, shrieking, "But it really happened that way! My mother liked it so what's wrong with you?! You only care about the market, not art! You only care about art, not the market! And one more thing—I never use exclamation poi—" at which point the phone machine cut her off. Needless to say, she never spoke to me again.

Why do we respond to comments about our work with either anger at ourselves or anger at others? Ego. At the bottom of these (self-) destructive responses is the foolish belief that we must be perfect for people to care about us. We think we must make absolutely no mistakes, and if we do, we're unlikable. Instead of realizing that making mistakes is a necessary part of every learning process, we either attack ourselves ("I'm a failure! I have no reason to live!"), or we kill the messenger ("You just don't know what it's like to work for days on a story! You're a narrow-minded, ignorant literary snob!"). It's as if we imagine that readers are reading our personalities rather than our stories. So what if an incident in our stories "really happened," or our mother liked it. If the writing doesn't work, it doesn't work. As I suggested in the section on "Ego" in chapter two, when you're reading a book and something seems off, you don't think, "Well, I'll excuse the author's sloppiness because I guess it really happened that way." You simply lose track of the story, or close the book. Our work is not us any more than our children are us, or a tune we're whistling is us. Our work is something we've created, something we can nurture and develop until at last it reaches maturity, something we don't need—and shouldn't expect—to get right on any particular deadline.

This craving to be perfect is, to be blunt, silly. No one expects that the first time he picks up a violin, or even after the first five years of practice on the violin, he'll be able to compose a great symphony. He may *want* this, but he knows he has to work up to it. Yet somehow, if that aspiring violinist picks up a pen instead of a bow, he believes he should be perfect, if not the first day, then the first year, or with the first novel. When I tell this to students, they say, "That's not a good analogy. I've been using words all my life, so it's not like I have to learn a whole new vocabulary." But in fact, it *is* a reasonable analogy. You may have been using words, but unless you've been using them on paper *and* you have been using them to tell stories, you are, when you write, essentially speaking a whole different language. Great photographers, though they use a visual language, don't immediately metamorphose into great movie directors; great barbecue cooks, though they use the language of food, don't immediately metamorphose into great chefs. Apprenticeships are involved, and apprenticeships necessitate the willingness to make mistakes. To rephrase the discussion in "Feelings of Failure" in chapter two, you cannot learn to walk until you can accept, even embrace, the necessity of falling.

All that said, how do you learn to handle the criticism that you will inevitably face?

The Three Universal Remedies

These are the keys to surviving criticism, as well as to coping with almost every other impediment you will have to face as a writer.

1. Eliminate your ego.
2. Acquire patience.
3. Listen to your inner voice.

When you eliminate your ego (and, as a corollary, your pride), you accept that you are not perfect. This means that you can hear what people say about your work and recognize that they are not saying it about *you*. You and the work are separate, just as you and the bookcase you made last weekend are separate. Once you accept this, you can handle people's comments with aplomb rather than self-anger or defensiveness. (See "Ego" and "Pride" in chapter two.)

Patience allows you to receive criticism with grace. If, for instance, a friend points out that the ending of the story seems forced, you realize that you need not mope or eliminate your friend from your Christmas card list but get back to work. So, the story wasn't perfect this time around. So what? What's the hurry? Your only deadline is your own death. Before that, all the deadlines are artificial. (See "Patience" in chapter three.)

And when you listen to your inner voice, you know which criticisms to value and which to dismiss. You know that certain comments are pointing you in someone else's direction rather than your own, and so, although you will listen (and perhaps learn) from these comments, you need not act precisely on them. You also know that certain comments duplicate your inner voice—"Hey, I knew that paragraph was dull, too, only I just didn't bother to work on it." In addition to helping you sort out the more useful comments from the less useful, your inner voice can help you determine whose comments are truly about your work, and whose are more about envy, or some old grudge, or mere taste. Plus, your inner voice will tug at your shirt-sleeve when a critic offers a comment that initially seems off base but is, in fact, simply an inarticulate expression of something that is highly valuable; *Listen to this!* it'll say. *It's worded poorly, but what she's really trying to say is something you ought to hear.* (See "The Inner Voice" in chapter three.)

With these three remedies you will find that criticism isn't such a big deal. You can face it all, whether it be from friends, teachers, or editors. Some experienced writers call this developing a thick hide. But that seems misleading, since it encourages beginning writers to assume they need to get calloused, toughened. Rather than developing a rough exterior, I prefer to think of handling criticism as developing a healthy interior. Work on the inside. Then whatever happens on the outside, however disappointing, cannot debilitate or destroy you. You'll see that *they* don't have that power. You and you alone do.

DELUSIONS OF THE CREATIVE PROCESS

Like the first few months of a new romance, writing is so exhilarating that, when we're in the thick of it, we can easily lose our judgment. In romance, this blinding passion almost always leads to impetuous thoughts of commitment—*Let's get married! Let's get my name tattooed on your heart and your name on my backside! We are Romeo and Juliet, Dante and Beatrice—ranking right up there with the greatest lovers of all time! With the power of us together, we could never fail—we could take on the entire world!*

In love, our delusions almost always run to the glorious. Not so in writing. In writing, delusions go both to glory and to despair. Either we rocket into the heavens of:

This is magnificent! I'm a total genius! No one has ever written such an earth-shattering opus before! I will transcend mortality! I will be bigger than Shakespeare!

Or we slide into the pit of:

This is imbecilic. I'm a complete loser. No one has ever eked out such drek before. I could die of shame. I'll be as insignificant as roadkill.

Either way, we often get into a trance of misperception, in which the most extreme grandiosity or the most hangdog self-abnegation seems to make absolute sense. Occasionally we think both kinds of thoughts at the same time, and, oddly enough, such paradoxical thinking seems to make sense, too.

As soon as you realize you are experiencing these delusions, you can address them. The first point to remember is that delusions are part of the creative process. We create; therefore, we fantasize. That is, we are so accustomed to chiseling our own reality out of the raw material of everyone else's that we know how to see what others do not and hence may believe what the available evidence may not yet support. Others see a room; we see the intersection of planes, the ceiling giving birth to the walls, the walls embracing the floor. Others see our story; we see the clumsy sentences, the brain-dead characters, the luscious setting, the astonishingly original take on the central moral dilemma, the resonant final line, the phone call from the Pulitzer committee saying that everyone now sees we are so wise that the President of the United States would like us to let him know if we would become his advisor, the stupid transition in the third paragraph.

Probably all artists experience delusions as they create. *Delusions are normal in the creative process.* If you acknowledge this fact, you aren't as likely to be bowled over by them when they occur.

The next step is to recognize that there is nothing wrong with delusions per se, provided we remind ourselves that that's what they are—mental illusions that we are inventing about ourselves—and don't allow them to control our writing process. But you need to make a distinction between positive and negative delusions, since they affect us differently. Positive delusions are those that lead us to believe in our own glory (the *I'm a genius* brand of fallacy); negative delusions lead us to believe in our own ineptitude. Let's break down what each does to us.

Positive Delusions. I often think that positive delusions are almost necessary for the writing process, especially in the first few drafts, when we are conjuring something out of nothing and need the reassurance, however overblown, that we are spending our energies usefully. After all, if we didn't think the guests would have a riproaring time at the party next week, would we even bother to send out the invitations today? If we didn't think our child would become a happy, healthy grown-up, would we really want to conceive? It is a reality of human nature that we need the lure of an oasis to take off into the desert. Positive delusions keep us lumbering forward, convinced we are doing something so important and good that we have no choice but to press on.

The only disadvantage to positive delusions is when we cling to them during later drafts. That is, if we continue, when we are venturing into the revision stage of writing, in believing that we have produced work of such virtuosity that New York agents will kowtow at the very sight of our manuscript tumbling down from the transom. When such tenaciously positive delusions occur, we resist shredding the sections that don't work in our writing, let alone rethinking the entire piece. How could we? Our superlative creation *must* stay intact to preserve its brilliance. Pull out a single brick and you will mar the divine beauty of the work. It would be like touching up the Mona Lisa so we see orthodontia, inserting a rap beat into "The Itsy, Bitsy Spider," giving Sleeping Beauty a bad case of insomnia. A single stroke of the delete key, we are convinced, would indisputably annihilate everything.

To translate, this means we are clinging to our ego.

This is not an insurmountable problem. In fact, I advise my students: when you are writing a first draft, *be* a monomaniac. Yes. Go ahead. I give you permission. Think yourself God. Maybe even a new and improved God. Dream of making millions. Of installing a heated swimming pool in your ten-acre backyard. Of winning the National Book Award. Of being the first American to be knighted. Of unleashing such public loyalty that your every trip to Shop-Rite is accompanied by a ticker-tape parade. Puff up with hope. Wallow in delirious joy.

But when you set sail toward revision, throw your ego overboard. You cannot get anywhere with revision if you are too protective; send your God costume home from the parade so you can get on with the business of sweeping up the sidewalk. Only then will you be able to see what needs to be done to your story and be willing to roll up your sleeves and do it, regardless of how much time and effort it takes. (See comments on ego in "Handling Criticism," earlier in this chapter.)

Negative Delusions. These thoughts are another matter altogether. Believing that our work should be mailed down the sewer grate, that our talents will evoke ridicule from every passerby, that our characters are limp, pasty dimwits who blatantly mirror the same narcissistic traits that caused our wife to leave us—such thoughts are not useful. Not only are they bad for our self-esteem, but when we believe them, we clam up and don't finish our draft at all, whether it is a first or five-hundredth draft. Negative delusions are anchors. Only they don't just keep us moored to one spot; they tug us down, out of the light and oxygen, until we drown in our own self-disgust and despair.

Fortunately, negative delusions can be neutralized, and as with all other thoughts, this can be done methodically. First, as I discussed earlier in "Hearing Your Inner Voice," negative delusions are fears, not realities. Variations on the theme of *This stinks, I stink, the whole world stinks* are not logical thoughts and certainly not accurate perceptions. They are the result of twisted thinking. They are manifestations of fear.

This may take a while to see, but once you get even a glimmer of it, go right into combat. Don't delay. Arm yourself with patience, egolessness, the inner voice, and cognitive therapy techniques (see "Cognitive Therapy" in chapter six). Put in your minimum of seven hours a week. Use a process journal to keep track of how you are feeling and thinking. And, most importantly, do not stop. If you don't stop, *you cannot fail,* because you will simply, by sitting down to write day after day, have to improve. The only way you can know conclusively that those negative delusions are accurate is if you stop. Otherwise, there is always hope that you can prove those delusions wrong.

A friend recently told me, "The true mark of a person is how he handles his fear." We all feel the fear. We all have the delusions. Some of us ignore them and keep trying anyway. Others of us give in, which means the fear wins because we quit.

Fear doesn't mean you can't. Fear only means you think you can't.
But you can.

Writing is not pain. Writing is only work. Long and patient work in which you give yourself over to the process and come to understand yourself. Writing takes effort, and time, and courage, and faith. Give it all that, and then writing won't even be work; it will be a path to self-knowledge and growth, a journey not of fear but of pleasure.

COPING WITH ALONENESS

We write alone. Even if we are on a crowded subway or in a noisy living room, even if we have discussed the story with friends at the bar or the teacher at her desk, when we put down the words, we are doing so on our own.

Often, we write in a private place—our bedroom, our office before dawn. We might even remain in this private place for hours. Ideas pounce upon us, and no one is there to hear. We laugh, but only our ears will know. And when we have questions, or feel scared, or want a congratulatory hug, we just have ourselves, sitting in our chair.

Sometimes this aloneness is no trouble at all. We are so involved with our characters that we don't feel alone; we feel spirited and energized.

But sometimes we don't feel as involved. Maybe we're full-time writers who wish we had a spouse. Maybe we just don't care about our characters yet. Whatever the trigger, our aloneness turns into feelings of isolation. Our solitude becomes oppressive. No one knows we exist. Maybe no one *cares* we exist. We don't know how to bear the silence.

How do we accept the long stretches of being alone, which we *must* have to write, so that they don't interfere with our writing?

Writers have struggled with this dilemma throughout the ages. Some turn to alcohol, though their reward is even worse depression, erratic personality traits, and early death. Some leave their offices to visit with other writers. This sometimes works, though it can also lead to lunches that go on for the rest of the day.

So how do we cope?

First, we need to remember that feelings of aloneness are different from loneliness, though we often treat them as if they were the same. As I discussed in chapter two, loneliness is not about a lack of social interaction, but about how we feel in the company of ourselves.

Knowing this, we might want to examine whether our unease with aloneness is more about an ache for other people or about a desire to escape ourselves. If it's the former, read on. If it's the latter, refer back to the section on "Loneliness."

Beyond that, we need to find ways to make peace with the aloneness or, as I think of it, to accept the *solo* in solitude. Every writer has his or her own list of ways to do so. This, I've found over the years, is mine:

• Live with people you love. Whether this is family or friends, their presence will give you social interaction to look forward to.

• If you can't or don't want to live with others, make social plans in advance—to occur *after* your writing time (all of it) is done. Again, this provides social compensation for all your time alone.

• Take frequent bathroom breaks. (This is easy if you are drinking a lot of tea or coffee.) When you are away from the desk, pause to look into the bathroom mirror. Yes, it's you, but it's the external you, which is a different version from the you you've spent the last hour with.

• Talk to yourself.

• Take breaks to call people on the phone. Whenever I have questions, I call friends who are knowledgeable on those subjects or I call libraries. A brief chat about the varieties of plastic egg cartons or the intricacies of legal procedures can do wonders toward making me feel reconnected with the world and refreshed enough to reconnect with my characters.

• Take a quick break to leave a nice phone message for one or two people you care about. They'll feel good when they play them back them later, and you'll feel good when you think about them doing so.

• Send letters so you can receive mail in the middle of your session. If you don't already have correspondents, sign up with a pen pal agency and get some. E-mail serves the same purpose.

• If you are writing full-time, then when you have finished your writing for the day, leave the place where you write and exercise or run errands. Do this every day, even if it's just to go to the grocery store or circle the block. Cultivate acquaintances with people you regularly see, whether that be other dog walkers or the guy at the newsstand. Sometimes it just helps to know that your existence is acknowledged.

- Find talk radio stations you can tolerate and tune them in when you have finished working and need a voice around.
- Always keep books, magazines, and newspapers around to read when you have stopped working.
- Write harder. Then you'll forget yourself, and focus on others (your characters), anyway.

Aloneness need not be difficult to manage. With some effort and the right attitude, it can be enjoyed. Then you'll be able to face it in other situations, and you'll be happier for knowing that you have such resourcefulness and strength.

CHAPTER EIGHT

WHEN YOU'RE STUCK

Sometimes, of course, the writer has made it through all the prelim-
inary heats—finding solutions to logistic challenges, learning how
to read as a writer, developing a fondness for the word No—but when
he finally gets on the field, the starting gate won't open, or halfway
down the track his legs buckle.

Being stuck—or writer's block, as this condition is commonly
called—can hit any writer at any age and at any stage. Henry Roth
published the acclaimed novel *Call It Sleep* in his twenties, then tumbled into a severe writer's block that lasted over fifty years. Humor
writer Fran Lebowitz is renowned for her writer's block, which
stretched across a few decades. During the last several years of
Truman Capote's life, he claimed to be working on the book *Answered
Prayers*, but as the final manuscript has never been found, some have
speculated that he was actually too incapacitated by writer's block to
produce anything. (This would make sense, as he was despondent
over the widespread ostracism he suffered after a gossipy excerpt
from the book appeared in *Esquire*.) My own worst case of block
occurred after I had written four book-length works as a kid; suddenly
from age eighteen to twenty-four, I froze completely, and couldn't
have dredged a word of fiction out of my pen if I'd been kidnapped
and had to write a story for my ransom.

Why do we get stuck? There are many reasons, but almost all of
them come down to fear. We are afraid what others will think of our
ideas, or our talent, or our chutzpah, or our intelligence, or our
money-making capacity. They will conclude we are no good, which
will be, we imagine, the proof that we are indeed no good. So we can't
do for fear of finding out that we, well, can't do. Hence, we do nothing.

Often, beginning writers who are stuck think that all they need is some kind of verification of their competence, and then they can get going. I have had countless unpublished students tell me that, if only they could get something published, they would become the prolific writers they know they really are inside. So insistent are these students that publication is their holy grail that they grow furious when I tell them that publication is a false god; it will not unlock them. "You just don't know!" one snapped at me, her eyes tearing as she confronted me in a school corridor. "*You've* been published. You *know* you're good. I'm *never* going to get there." I told her she was mistaken; I was on intimate terms with writer's block, as most writers are. In fact, some of the most celebrated cases of writer's block have happened to published authors, particularly after they publish a book to great acclaim and need to come up with another. (This subset of writer's block is fairly common for successful first-time authors, for whom it is called "sophomore slump" or "sophomore jinx." The expectations of them seem so high, they can't move forward one word.)

What gets you out of being stuck is not external. Writer's block comes from within and as a result can be healed only from within.

The first thing you can do when you're stuck is to remind yourself of the cyclical nature of the writing process. Writing works a lot like the seasons: You do tremendous work at some times, producing insightful, exciting creations that seem as if they will keep writing themselves forever. Then your energy tapers off, or your ideas come to feel rigid and dry. You enter a phase of not writing, of simply sitting around, feeling dark. And then—voila!—something spins back into place, and you can get going again.

When we're writing actively and regularly, we're caught up in a writer's flow. When we're hitting the bumps, slowing down, and abandoning the car, we've hit writer's block.

This cycle happens to all writers, but the duration varies from person to person and from incident to incident. Some writers may experience block for only a five-minute gap in their thirty-year careers. Others may have thirty-year blocks with only a five-minute burst of flow. Most writers hit block occasionally. Block itself is not the problem; the frequency and steadfastness with which it occurs are.

If you are enduring long-term or, more likely, habitual blocks, you may feel there is no way out. There is. Let's start by breaking down the cycle of the writing process to understand more about why we sometimes enter winter and how to get ourselves into spring.

When we're writing actively and effortlessly, when we're in a period of flow, we can't imagine how we were ever in block or that we might topple into it again. Writing is so much pleasure! we tell ourselves. It makes all the difficulties in the rest of our lives seem easy to handle; in fact, it seems to remove the difficulties from the rest of our lives. When we're writing with flow, we feel such a sense of hope about our talent and the prospects for our career that optimism permeates everything in our lives. The promising date who doesn't call back? Sure, it's a bummer, but hey, we've got this spectacular story unfolding before our eyes, showing us how smart and witty and sexy we are inside, *so we believe we're going to be okay*. The bill collector who keeps calling? Yeah, we still fret about how to get greenbacks into his hand, but with this fascinating novel on our screens we know we're competent and bankable, *so we believe we're going to be okay*. When we're in flow, nothing can dent us. Our writing sails us over our worries by reminding us that there is more to life than our worries. Plus, it gives us all the proof we need, aside from anything an outside source might say, that we should keep going.

But then, sometimes, we feel a change. *I'm stuck*, we think, and we skid into despair. Seldom, however, does this have to do with our writing itself. Deemphasize the *stuck*; the trouble is virtually always with the *I*. That is, stuckness comes from a negative shift in how we're seeing ourselves, whether as people or as writers. Instead of believing we're going to be okay, we begin to feel we're failures, that nothing we do will work out, that we are destined to be zeroes. We believe this so completely that we lock up inside, and can't give ourselves the freedom to be imperfect on the page. Therefore, we can't write.

When I was trudging through my six-year writer's block from eighteen to twenty-four, I didn't know any of this. I truly believed I couldn't write because I had no ideas, and because I wasn't thick-skinned enough to take criticism from editors. (As I mentioned in the "Introduction," just before my last day of high school, a teacher sensitively edited three of my stories with me; I was so mortified to see I had not been perfect that, instead of recognizing I just needed to do more work, I believed I would never make it.) I thought the problem was in my abilities as a writer.

Only many years later, long after I'd returned to writing, did I see what had really been going on. At age sixteen, two years before the block entombed me, I had undergone an extreme and sudden change in my family circumstances: My mother impetuously married an ex-con she'd just met in a bar and then went on the lam with him, disappearing for seven years. I was taken in by a charitable boarding school, and then a charitable college, but for a long time I remained an emotional wreck. I felt unworthy of a mother's love, which is a deep cut indeed. My shock and anger were so great I turned them on myself, telling myself I was no good, meant to be kicked around like dirt. During my first few years in this situation I still managed to write, but eventually my debilitated self-image seeped all the way through my spirit, and I couldn't manage to do any writing at all, with the exception of school papers. Each day the problem would multiply; since I couldn't write, I would tell myself that I wasn't, as I'd always believed, a writer, and the more strenuously I insisted to myself I was not a writer, the more certain I was that I couldn't write. Not writing proved to me that I was not a writer, rather than simply letting me know that I was in a bad patch, a time when I needed to process my life by living instead of by producing. Not writing didn't mean that I needed not to write; not writing, I believed, meant that I was a not.

After college, still believing these distortions, I went on with my life. I got jobs unrelated to writing, surrounded myself with friends, and met the man who became my first husband. I also, after much agonizing, tracked down my mother and reestablished a relationship, and realized that what had happened had nothing to do with my personality or degree of worthiness, but with her insecurity and her own demons.

This realization took a while to sink in. In the meantime, I came to feel loved and appreciated in both my private and working lives and, as a result, to feel better about myself.

And so, when I sat down to write again (a year after I'd remet my mother), I found my block was gone. This wasn't because I understood literature that much better or had learned dramatically new approaches to opening a story. My talent hadn't changed. My knowledge of books hadn't changed in any monumental way. My feelings about myself had.

All the other writer's blocks I've heard about are, in essence, the same story. This even applies to one of the most common kinds of block, the post-first-book paralysis. Yes, the long-struggling author is thrilled to be finally thought of so highly by an editor, ecstatic to be given this tremendous opportunity to prove himself at last, but underneath it all, he may wonder if he is, in fact, a fraud. Perhaps the editor is deluded. Perhaps the author is not great at all, as the editor believes, nor even cruising toward great, but is instead doomed, as are all charlatans, to poke around forever in some cul de sac of mediocrity. As stuck as his uncle with the dishonorable discharge and succession of foolhardy investments. Such twisted thinking, which encourages the young writer to believe that his first success will be his last, can lead to shame, guilt, and feelings of failure, which in turn may prompt him to avoid the page or even the world in general. As a blocked first novelist friend once lamented to me, "I hate walking down the street, because my neighbors keep asking how the next book is coming. Maybe I should just crawl into a cave and go away."

How can we keep writing when we can barely keep our chins up? How can we resume our productivity when our thinking has become so coiled and fractured that we feel flawed, fraudulent, and perhaps even worthless?

Essentially, when I pulled myself out of my writer's blocks, I did so by applying the concepts of cognitive therapy, which I discussed in chapter six. That is, I recognized that I was believing highly negative things about myself, most of which came down to some variation of *I'm no good*. I'm a phony. I'm a dummy. I'm a flash in the pan. I'm past my prime. I suck. Then I came to see that these thoughts were not facts but misbeliefs. I could then dismantle my negative belief system, release myself from my self-condemnation, and get back to letting myself write.

In the example above, I did this by developing love in my life through friendships and romance. This gave me the evidence I needed that I *was* good. At my present stage of life, however, I avoid block by applying cognitive therapy methodically and immediately if I sense I am falling into negative thoughts about myself as a writer or a person. This is a much more effective and efficient way to keep myself moving forward, since it doesn't rely on others. And it feeds on itself: Because I can address and correct my distortions on my own, I add to my sense of self-worth. I am untangling my thoughts on my own; therefore, I can keep writing on my own. Independent healing begets confidence, which begets writing. You only stay stuck when you dislike you.

I urge all my blocked students to keep a process journal (described in "Warming Up," chapter six) and read up on cognitive therapy. I also urge them to relax and work on the Three Universal Remedies: (1) Eliminate your ego; (2) Acquire patience; and (3) Listen to your inner voice. (These were discussed in "Handling Criticism," chapter seven.) And for the writers struggling with post-first-book paralysis, I discuss the solutions in a section of chapter ten, "The Difficulties and Gifts of Success," under the subheading "Writing—The Tough Stuff."

Put together, *this is all you need to get yourself out of block.*

But perhaps you've been reading this and thinking, Well, that's not *me.* My problem is technical. I simply don't know *how* to get the stolen porpoise through the streets of Tampa to the aquarium where Lorna the marine biologist sits in tears beside the empty tank. *That's* why I'm stuck, not any emotional mumbo jumbo. Simon, you're not helping me with that.

So for those of you who insist it's all technical, here's a breakdown of the three times when you're most likely to feel blocked—none of which, as you'll see, result from purely technical reasons—and the nontechnical approaches you can take to address each.

BLOCKED FROM THE BEGINNING OF THE DRAFT

You have a fabulous idea for a piece of fiction, yet you can't get yourself to start writing it. You are baffled by this. Maybe you can see the whole story—the saloon doors slapping together, the lone saddled mare wandering into town, the glint in the gold tooth of the corrupt sheriff—so clearly that your inability to write it mystifies you. Or maybe you have a gem of an idea but no sense of the setting in which it should go. Or maybe you have monumentally ambitious stylistic and thematic goals yet no characters nor even a glimpse of a scene.

Whatever the problem, you can't write more than a page or two of the beginning. What is going on here?

You might be caught up in wanting to eat the entire banquet in one humongous gulp instead of, as you must, a single, human-sized mouthful at a time. If you already see a lot of the story in your mind or a bright, shining central idea or theme, you might be fearful that you can't get your words up to that level of skill or do justice to that central vision. You know you must write one word and then another, but you are impatient to complete the great plan. Single words—

even paragraphs—seem too time-consuming, too onerous, too *boring*. Not only that, but they could lead you astray, divert you from your desired scheme. Or they could lead you to define characters and scenes that you would rather leave undefined, since defining them might drag your monumentally ambitious goals down to the level of the microcosm and the everyday. And the process? The revision? Ach! It'll take too long to crawl to what you can already see. What trouble. You simply can't get psyched up for any of it. You just want to take a nap instead. Your imagination is so overwhelmed by the task ahead that it would rather lie down and get a nice forty winks.

At this point, you will probably do one of two things. You will either quit writing entirely, in which case you're not likely to be reading this book. Or you will decide that your problem is not fear or impatience, but that you just don't know what to do. You simply need more information. That's it. You need to look at completed books, you decide, searching (depending on your dilemma) for either data or examples. If only you could spend some time reading up on your subject matter, or studying books written in a style similar to your own, or perusing stories to stimulate some epiphany of setting or character, or scouring biographies of authors who wrote novels as ambitious as the one you're planning—then you'd have either your missing data or your model of the "right" way, and then you'd get unstuck.

This is a stock response to beginning-the-draft block. Instead of acknowledging their fears and applying egolessness, patience, and the inner voice, many writers try to overcome beginning-the-draft block by reading a lot. Not *writing* at the same time, since that is too scary. But reading only. They tell themselves that by reading, they will see how other writers did it, and so will see how *they* can do it. Or they will become experts in the information they need, and so be able to go forth.

Between my first and second books, I believed this too. I recognized I was terrified of starting a second book—a novel, no less—and so I began reading and reading other novels. Over the months, my list of must-read novels grew, and the more I read, the further my start date receded. This might have gone on for years had I not had a conversation one night with a friend who for seven years had been unable to write her dissertation. She asked how my novel was coming, and I told her I was reading a lot of novels to see how to write a novel. She laughed and said she'd been reading a lot of dissertations to see how to write a dissertation. Then she added what a teacher of hers had advised: "Every piece of writing is unique, whether novels or dissertations. Yours will be too. You can read as many other novels or dissertations as you want, but all they're going to show you is how other people did their novels or dissertations. You won't be able to do yours until you just start to do it."

Don't use reading as an excuse for not trying to write. Reading might give you that *ker-pow!* of inspiration and it might not, but if you're not writing at the same time, you'll never see the inspiration evolve into work on the page.

It is tempting to give yourself tasks that you *must* complete before you start. Sure, you might need to do some research on how peasants lived during the Russian revolution, or on how the inside of a nuclear reactor looks during refueling. Or you might need to see how Faulkner began his book with a retarded boy so you can make allusions to it in your book about a retarded boy. But first drafts are not about getting all the details right. First drafts are about getting the basic story out. If you give yourself a slew of must-do chores first, you'll never get going. You might think you are on your way, but in reality all you are doing is getting your chores done and tricking yourself into believing that you are writing. Unfortunately, once the chores are done, your fears will not have gone away. In fact, they might even be worse, because you'll have too much to measure up to.

Just write, one page and day at a time. If it comes out "wrong," work on it later. First drafts are your time to make mud pies and get all dirty. You get stuck before you begin them only if you aren't willing to be patient with the process and accept that you will need to revise.

This is true no matter how you conceive the piece. Neither the well-visualized story nor the great central idea story will materialize unless you sit down and begin. Maybe your writing is far, far away from capturing your desired vision. That's fine. If you keep working and revising, you'll either capture your vision or write your way into a new and more interesting one than you'd originally imagined. All of which means you need to start—not just so you can get the project underway but, more importantly for your block, so that you can begin to diminish your fears.

Ditto for the ambitious plans. Many beginning writers can't get going because they want to write a novel that encapsulates all the knowledge of civilization, plus answers every question about humanity that every great philosopher has ever pondered. All these writers can see when they peer into their writing future is a massive palace of literature, an extraordinary creation that will make *War and Peace* look as interesting as a grocery list, a book that, once entered, will transform the reader like a dinner with the Buddha.

In other words, the goal is so big, and you're so small, you just can't brave the feat.

Again, the only way to do it is to start. And start small. *Very* small. Just a paragraph or a page. Or start with a tiny subject—a mouse scrabbling for a crumb beneath a parked stagecoach, instead of a king getting decapitated. Maybe start with a minor character or an image of the moon. Then move to the next step. One. Thing. At. A. Time. Move slowly. Don't get it "right." Just get it out. Right can come later. Out is all you need now. Producing a complete draft, however clumsy and silly it reads, can help reduce your fears, as it will render you feeling somewhat more in control.

Beginning-the-draft block is most likely to occur when writers feel under a deadline. If the deadline is external, an editor or teacher waiting with tapping foot for the chapter, you still need to apply the one-step-at-a-time approach, and you still need to give yourself room to make a mess. You can always revise. If, however, the deadline is internal—you think you should have a story done by now, you'd better have that novel written by the time you're forty or else!—then look back at the discussion of "Patience" in chapter three.

WHEN STUCK IN LATER DRAFTS

So you've got your first draft, maybe even your second or third. But you're not happy with it. Perhaps you know where you want it to end up, perhaps you don't—either way, you're not sure how to get there.

This is the one instance in which your block might be due to technical trouble. Which means that your trouble may be quite easily solved by revision. Many books cover revision in great detail, and I suggest you refer to them to understand the process more thoroughly than I can explain here. But they probably won't cover the fundamental attitudes that are necessary to face and proceed with revision, and that's what this section is about.

First, bone up on the Three Universal Remedies. That is, constantly and consciously work on keeping your ego out of the process. Constantly and consciously remind yourself of the need for patience. Constantly and consciously tune into the concerns of your inner voice. (See "Handling Criticism" in chapter seven.)

Then you need to work at accepting that the text is fluid. A lot of our resistance to revision comes from some bizarre feeling that once we've put the words down, they're sacred. It's ridiculous, but we do it again and again. We begin a story with a sense of openness, the blank page some uncharted ocean that is ours alone to frolic in. But as soon as we put anything on the page, we lose that sense of freedom and spaciousness, as though the ocean has turned to solid rock. But the words are *not* solid rock. The words are fluid. Your entire story is fluid. By that I mean infinitely malleable, variable, fixable. This applies from the level of the word to the level of character to the level of the plot itself.

I think we switch from ocean to rock because we fear we won't be able to come up with a better solution. In the first draft of my novel, which I spent two years revising, I lost control of the storyline fairly early in the book and spent the next seven hundred pages following all kinds of subplots and characters that, I eventually realized, were unnecessary and in fact prevented me from figuring out the plot and characters I really needed. I was loath to cut anything, and so I didn't. Instead, I let the novel sit like a prop on the corner of my desk, a concrete Mt. Everest that I couldn't imagine climbing.

In the meantime, I turned to other writing projects and settled on one that was (thank you, god) a rewrite of a previously unsuccessful story. I had worked on this story for years, altering the ending, switching from first to third person, but essentially leaving most of it intact—solid rock. I decided to turn the story into a screenplay, which meant that I needed to rethink the structure entirely, add characters, adjust the pace, externalize the ending, and so on. Luckily, it had been several years since I'd worked on that story, so I no longer cared about any particular paragraph or development. In fact, I no longer cared about anything except the basic idea. The text suddenly became fluid; I saw I could do anything I wanted with it. So I extracted what I cared about from the story, dropped the rest, and—abracadabra—found I *could* turn my handkerchief into a rabbit and quite an exquisite one at that.

Thus empowered, I returned to my novel. I now knew that I needed to see text as fluid. That is, I needed to address *every element of the piece*, not just plot and characters but also structure and tone and length and a zillion other things. I had previously seen this as impossible: They were *my* words; *I* had worked at putting them there; what if I lost something vital? I tried to counter this attitude with egolessness. So what if they were my words, right? They weren't working, so out they should go.

Still, it was a novel, the first novel I had written as an adult, and unlike when I'd rewritten the failed story into a screenplay, I found that I needed some help in making this attitudinal shift. In effect, I needed a technical crutch. Then I remembered that I had once read about a writer who threw into a dresser drawer everything he scissored out of his early drafts. I decided to follow this example and see if it helped, though I decided to use not a drawer, but a computer file. I called it CUTS, and whenever I hit a section of writing that I thought I might need to sever from the novel, I simply tossed it in there. Almost instantly, I lost any residual squeamishness about revising my novel, because I knew that if I wanted to reuse those sections, they still existed. This, in turn, reinforced my new ability to see my text as fluid. I could cut, I could retrieve, I could add, I could cut what I added. The novel melted from solid rock back to a liquid form, one that I could pour and repour into new shapes and sizes. I felt freer than I'd ever felt before. After twenty-five years of writing, I finally felt that I was learning to write.

That, however, was not the only new attitude I needed to adopt to stay unstuck. I also needed to recognize that there are many levels of revision. That is, what I had *thought* was revision—trimming the ending, changing from present to past tense, making a red dress blue—was only one level of revision, and the final one at that. Revision can be an all-encompassing Sherman's army that mows down everything except the name of the town, or it can be a dainty spring breeze that does little besides ruffle the petals. Sometimes all that's needed is a spring breeze. But in the case of that novel, I needed to attack with much more powerful force.

After I sold my novel, I found that people began asking me about revision. How could I have reconstructed my novel so drastically? They knew about revision, but when they pruned their endings, or made a red dress blue, their novels didn't really get any stronger. What did I know that they didn't?

I explained that there are different levels of revision, and, in striving to elaborate, I came up with three basic divisions of the process. These are, in my own personal terminology, cosmetic changes, surgical strikes, and major overhauls.

Cosmetic Changes. (Also known as polishing.) This is the dainty spring breeze level of revision, the tiny things you change here and there. You want to change Cinderella's slipper from gold to glass, for instance, so you erase one word and substitute the other. Or maybe you realize that two sentences make the same point. Listen: "On that June morning, beneath the trumpeting rays of the sun, roses blushed into bloom, frogs sprang skyward from sleepy crouches, and seedlings do-si-doed with adolescent glee. It was a beautiful day." Obviously, "It was a beautiful day" merely recapitulates what was just illustrated and therefore is unnecessary. Being a careful writer, you cut it. Cosmetic changes are the easiest kind of changes and, as a result, are what beginning writers usually think is meant by revision. Fix a word here and there, alter hair color from blonde to brunette, and the story is finished. However, this is frequently the final, not the first, level of revision *no matter how brilliant a writer you are.* This is one of the most major attitudinal shifts that a writer must make. We all want to think that our stories need only cosmetic changes and, in fact, that cosmetic changes are what is meant by the term "revision." But cosmetic changes are only the finishing touches. Accepting this early in your writing career will make your life much easier.

Surgical Strikes. These are similar to cosmetic changes, except instead of working on the level of the word or sentence, they're on the level of the paragraph or section. Maybe in the middle of your Cinderella story you have a lovely flashback about Cinderella's days in the Girl Scouts, and how she earned her botanical merit badge while gathering strawberries in a meadow. The scene has nothing to do with the story of Cinderella, and so despite its lyrical appeal, eventually you come to recognize it's superfluous and cut it. Or let's say you've organized the story so Cinderella goes to the ball and comes home and returns to being a servant girl. You need to have the prince rescue her, but you can't figure out how to get them together again. Finally revision lightning strikes, and you realize you need to introduce an element that's not in your story, so you invent the device of the glass slipper, which you then go back and weave all through the story. The surgical strike, then, is a bit more challenging than a cosmetic change, because it means giving up something substantial that was in your first draft or putting in something substantial that had not been there previously.

Major Overhauls. This is Sherman's army, the most formidable level of revision. Let's say you started writing a story about sad, lonely Cinderella, a servant girl to her stepmother and stepsisters. But shortly after the first page, you veered off into having Cinderella meet a Martian and then shifted to Mars and spent time with the Grack family, and you needed to get Cinderella to Mars but didn't have a rocket in the story so you just figured, *Screw it, no one will notice,* and put her on Mars, and while we're at it, let's stick that Girl Scout scene in somewhere. Eventually you realize that what you've written doesn't tell a good story, and that for it to do so, you need to blow up your first draft and start again from scratch. This is the TNT approach to revision, and unfortunately this is necessary much more often than we might like. With my collection of short stories I never did a major overhaul, but I sure did with my novel, and in fact major overhaul accounted for most of my two years of revision. With major overhaul, you shove dynamite into the text, detonate, and rescue only those shards of the story that will work. This is by far the most arduous level of revision, but once you've done it, you feel that you can conquer anything.

Attitude Changes

Almost every piece of fiction initially needs at least a surgical strike, if not a major overhaul. It is important to recognize that these earlier stages of revision, though seemingly overwhelming at first, actually take a shorter period of time than the later stage of revision, cosmetic changes. This is because major overhauls and surgical strikes deal with larger, and hence fewer, elements; cosmetic changes deal with all the minute elements, and so you have many.

A few other attitude changes are worth mentioning here. The first is that revision is a cyclical process. One round of bettering your draft is only one round. It may take you many rounds before the story (or paragraph, or sentence) is done. This doesn't mean you're stupid or untalented. It means you're normal. Hilma Wolitzer, writing about revision in her essay "Twenty Questions," says, "Do you revise? Is the sun going to set today? One of the great *pleasures* of writing is revision, the second and third and fourth chance you hardly ever get in any other area of your life." I have read an interview with Amy Tan in which she mentioned that she revised *The Joy Luck Club* twelve times. I have read that Jean Auel revised the beginning of *The Clan of the Cave Bear* thirty times. As for myself, I revise so many times I don't count. Revision is a fact of life.

Also, realize there is no one correct way to revise anything. Revision is about exploring some possibilities out of an infinite selection of possibilities and finding the solutions that work best for your particular story and appeal most to your inner voice. But there is no single, perfect answer to every revision problem. There is no "correct" or "right" writing; there is only good writing. The more creative your solutions are to your revision problems, the better your writing will be.

And finally, recognize that sometimes you are too close to the material. This tends to happen when we are writing about something that is autobiographical; we know so many of the details and have so many mixed feelings that we can't see straight enough to get the piece into a workable shape. If this applies to you, consider letting some of your story deviate from your original plan. If you are white, maybe make the character who is based on you black, or if you are twenty, change your character to forty. Drop details that are there because you want them, but that you don't need. Shift locations, plot developments, number of major players in the story. Develop different revelations. Don't stick to fact. Fiction isn't journalism. It's fiction.

That's all I know about helping yourself get on with revision. Try following these tips—not just for a day or two but for weeks or months. No experiment can work overnight, and certainly not one as profound as changing your attitudes about revision.

If, however, you try all this and still feel stuck with revising, you might want to spend some time away from the piece, during which you live your life and/or write other things. Then, when you return, you might be able to see the piece with fresh eyes and feel less attached to your words, and so be able to go back through these suggestions again with greater ease, satisfaction and, possibly, success.

WHEN UNABLE TO WRITE AT ALL

You have stories you want to start and stories half revised. And you can't face any of them. Maybe you can sit down at the desk, but you can't get a single word out of your pen. Maybe this has gone on for weeks, or months, or years. What can you do to escape from this hell?

This condition is blatantly not technical. Of course you could write a word—even meaningless words. But you feel you can't write at all. You feel completely frozen. You are a writer trapped in amber.

Usually this occurs when a writer has been trying to conquer a specific novel or story that has proven elusive. One of my friends has been blocked for five years because she can't face a half-written novel and can't seem to let herself begin anything else. I've had recurring bouts of block over a magical romantic novel I've never been able to write.

My solution and the solution I recommend to my students? *Write something else.* It doesn't matter what. Letters to correspondents. A journal. Fairy tales for your kids. Your mother's words, verbatim, about how she met your father. Haiku. Content doesn't matter. Beauty of language doesn't matter. The only thing that counts is the act of writing itself. Your writing muscles will never be able to handle the decathlon if you don't first let them pick up a fork so you can eat your peas and carrots. Just write anything that appeals to you. Write until you remember the fun and pleasure of writing. Then keep writing some more.

Eventually, you'll write your way into a place where you've never been before. Maybe that will be a rewarding pen pal relationship with your five-year-old niece. Maybe it will be a career as an ad copywriter. Maybe it will be a single prose poem that you can insert in your Valentine's Day cards.

Whatever it is, it's still writing.

In other words, if you can't do it at all, try some other it. You might find it's just as worthwhile as your original goal, if not more so.

I still haven't written the magical romantic novel, but in the interest of surviving the blocks it inspired, I've written another novel, dozens of stories, and this book. I now know I'll write that novel someday, because I've written myself into a state of faith. And in the meantime, I've been productive and improving, so that when I finally manage to write it, I'll do a much better job than I would have done before.

PART THREE
BECOMING
AN AUTHOR

CHAPTER NINE

STEPPING INTO THE PUBLISHING WORLD

Now we come to the stage that, to one degree or another, most writers view with a sense of apprehension: sending their work into the world. If the work gets accepted, as we all hope it will, we know we will be thrilled. If the work gets rejected, as we pray it won't, then we think we will be sad at best and crushed at worst.

We feel apprehensive for a variety of reasons. Fear of embarrassment is a main one. A beginning writer might feel distress over what his friends or family will think if he can't sell his work, particularly if he feels pressure from them to justify his time and effort: "What? You've been writing for (fill in the blank) years and you *still* haven't sold anything? Maybe it's time you gave up."

For the experienced writer, embarrassment has more to do with people *in* publishing, as he frets over editors and agents and reviewers—people who are no longer strangers but now business associates and maybe friends—losing faith in him because his new work isn't eliciting the excitement his older work once did.

Another reason we are anxious about submitting our work is a concern about how rejection or a less enthusiastic or lucrative response than we desire might affect our moods. We fear the growth of bitterness or maybe a shift in our character toward the more cynical and unhappy. We have fueled ourselves through the writing process with our optimism and faith; we are concerned that rejection might revive our pessimism or turn our faith inside out into distrust of the process and doubts about ourselves. And, of course, no one wants to feel even a trickle, let alone a flow, of disappointment or sorrow.

Submission derives from the root *submit*, which means to yield to the authority of another. In submitting our work, we sometimes feel that we are in a submissive position. We think others have power over us. We think, *Please, please want us, or something inside us might die.*

Or so we fear.

But submission fears, and fears of all aspects of stepping into the publishing world, can be combatted. They are their own battles but in many ways are no different from all the other emotional battles you have already fought through. This is as true for the beginner as for the advanced writer. There are times when these skirmishes are easier to enter; others, when they seem excruciating. But it can be done. In fact, it *must* be done, if you are to keep going as a writer.

This chapter begins with a discussion of how to get through the experience of rejection. If you see that what you are feeling is typical, you will get through this time with no more cynicism than you originally possessed and no reduction in your literary libido. Indeed, you will persevere—and do so with a lot more wisdom about yourself, humanity, and the world. The second half of this chapter addresses the business side of writing and how to handle your paperwork and people contact with professionalism. By the end of the chapter, you should be able to hear "No" without letting it drive you into anything other than continued persistence and know how to handle yourself in the business arena with confidence.

REJECTION

It begins with the mailbox.

Whether it is our fiftieth book or our first story, we must mail the thing out. We slip our manuscript into an envelope and make our way to the mailbox, knowing that we have toiled; applied egolessness, patience, and our inner voice; sacrificed a season of dinner parties and sleep; worshipped on the altar of revision. We know that what we have is good. Not only that, but our trusted readers agree that it is good. So it is with hope that we let the blue handle of the mailbox swing closed and return home, eager to receive a response.

Sometimes, we get what we want: The editor phones us and in an ebullient voice announces, *Incredible story. Where have you been hiding out, Ms. So-and-So? I'll take it!* Or, better yet, the agent calls and, in a voice fairly cracking with ecstasy, squeals, *Five places are dying to have it—we're going to auction!*

But sometimes we receive a rejection letter. Most likely, then, some degree of frustration will descend. If we're feeling resilient and are keeping in mind those famous tales of other writers' perseverance—Patrick Dennis' 15 rejections before the sale of *Auntie Mame,* Madeleine L'Engle's 30 rejections before *A Wrinkle in Time* caught an editor's eye, Robert Pirsig's 121 rejections before *Zen and the Art of Motorcycle Maintenance* was accepted—we immediately stick the manuscript in a new envelope to send to another publication. But even if we go through those steps and tell ourselves that rejection isn't the worst calamity we will encounter in our lives, that perhaps it will strengthen our character, we might still feel the sting. Maybe softly, mild enough to need no social or psychological Bactine, but still present.

For some writers this experience leads to extreme reactions. A poet who had previously won a grant from the NEA became so disheartened by her failed attempts to get her book of poetry published that for a long time she stopped writing entirely. A writer of three celebrated novels was mired in such shock when his fourth book wasn't accepted that he almost dropped out of his marriage. And, of course, there is the well-known case of John Kennedy Toole, so despondent over his failure to sell his novel *A Confederacy of Dunces* that he killed himself. The manuscript, which was inherited upon his death by his determined and resourceful mother, was published a decade later to outstanding critical acclaim, winning the Pulitzer Prize posthumously for its author, but Toole himself apparently felt nothing but an increasingly morbid sense of discouragement.

Like most writers, I have suffered greatly over some of my own rejections. When five publishers turned down my second book (and first novel), I pulled it from further submission. I felt so dejected that I did little but mope about for four months, not even getting out of bed some days. I washed the dishes, read the newspaper, and occasionally paid bills from my savings account, but beyond that I accomplished nothing.

Clearly, my book's inability to entice a publisher had set off a depression in me, and as frequently happens during depression, I engaged in illogical thoughts. I believed that I was talentless, that I'd deluded myself into thinking I'd written a good book but that in reality I was incapable of writing one. I imagined that when my name came up in the publishing world, it evoked snickers and rolling eyes.

My ten-year college reunion was, coincidentally, scheduled at the end of these four months. I tried to prepare myself to face my classmates and admit that, no, I hadn't "made it" as a writer after all. I dragged myself to my old campus, and there I meandered over to the office of my former advisor. Fortunately, Professor Kilbride happened to be rummaging through his papers. He was pleased to see me, and when I broke down and tearfully admitted that my current book hadn't sold, he did the last thing I expected and the first thing I needed: He laughed. Not at me but over how seriously I was taking this development in my life.

Suddenly I saw how ridiculous I was being; this rejection was nothing more than a rejection by these particular publishers of this particular book. It was not a confirmation of my worthlessness as a person or as a writer. Nor was it even a confirmation that *this* book was worthless. Professor Kilbride then added that he failed all the time in his attempts to accomplish things. As I mentioned in chapter two, he told me that feelings of failure are normal, almost to be expected, and that the higher we strive, the more we will fail, because the closer we get to the top, the fewer doors there are and the greater the competition to open them. To be successful, we must learn to overcome feelings of failure *because they will strike us, inevitably.*

I realized then that a lot of my problem had been my belief that no one else was as miserable about rejection as I. I thought I was alone with my feelings of failure. But after that conversation with my professor, I stopped seeing myself as an anomaly. *All people experience failure at all stages of their lives.* Our task is to learn how we, given our unique strengths and interests, can face the failure and keep going instead of letting it paralyze us. Overcoming failure is just another fact of life.

And it helps not to take it all so seriously.

Soon after this encounter, I began writing again. Not the troublesome novel, but other projects, both new and old. This return to the writing process, and consequently to the wizardly powers of writing, proved enormously reassuring. Yes, it does work, I realized, I am still a writer. After several months, I felt stronger and picked up the novel again. Two years of rewriting later I sold it, this time after it had been with an editor for less than two weeks.

As with most other aspects of writing, the first step in facing rejection is to acknowledge that it happens to everyone and that your feelings of being a failure are normal. You are not an exception. You have vast amounts of company. You just *feel* as if you are the only person to have suffered rejection, to think you are inadequate, to struggle with disappointment and shame. You are not.

Now that you understand that your feelings are normal, that the world is not out to get you, you can examine your thoughts more clearly. Use your process journal (see "Warming Up" in chapter six). See if the rejections are bringing up old thoughts about being dumb, or stubborn, or lazy, or whatever. Then, employing the cognitive therapy techniques discussed in chapter six, see if these are logical thoughts that can trigger a set of logical actions, or illogical thoughts that need to be countered by logical responses. It is quite possible that you are feeling like a failure not because you have *failed*, but because you believe, somewhere underneath, that you are deeply, conclusively a flop.

The final and most complicated step is to figure out a course of action. This falls into two major categories: action if you believe the editors who rejected your piece are wrong, and action if you believe they are right.

You believe the editors are wrong to reject your piece. If you have really worked your story before submitting it—employed egolessness, patience, and your inner voice—and you have polished every word hundreds of times to the point where you are absolutely certain that everything, from the most macro to the most micro of elements, is exactly as it should be, then you might have grounds to believe that the editors are "wrong"—i.e., that they should have accepted your great piece of writing simply because it was a great piece of writing.

Editors make decisions that are based on many factors beyond whether or not a piece is well written. A piece might be supremely well written and still get rejected if the editors feel that, given their tastes or needs, it is not appropriate for their publication. Perhaps they have just published a story set, as is yours, in a nursing home; or they are tired of stories set in a nursing home; or because of their sour relationship with their grandfather, they cringe at the very notion of a story set in a nursing home; or they believe that their audience is not interested in stories set in nursing homes. Or maybe they are so inundated by worthy stories that they simply lack the opportunity to print all the good ones they get. Or maybe your story is too long for their space restraints, or in the first person when they have a personal bias toward third, or has a sad ending when their market research indicates that their readers prefer happy endings.

In other words, if you believe that the publishers are wrong about the worth of your story, recognize that their rejection may have to do with the story's worth, but it also might have to do with other considerations or flukes.

You may not be able to figure out why your story wasn't taken. In fact, you will probably have no clue. This makes it hard to process the fact of the rejection and to determine if your perceptions of your story's value are accurate. But if you truly believe in your story (and, I must stress, *have a very good basis for such belief*), then you can proceed in any event, even without processing.

Proceeding in this case means figuring out what you can do to get this story published. Here you have several options.

1. Keep trying different editors.

2. Sit on it awhile until you meet an editor and then hand it directly to him/her.

3. Forget editors. Try contests. Try grants.

4. Rework the story in a new form (script, novel, etc.).

5. Write new work so you don't overemphasize the importance of this one piece.

6. Find other angles. Try to publish excerpts (useful only if your work is book-length). Speak to theatrical and film people about adaptations. Have someone use it as the basis of a song or a musical. Try editors abroad.

7. Do something no one else has done. Richard Brautigan became known as a poet in San Francisco by typing his poetry onto pieces of paper that he sold on the street corner for a dollar. The editor of this book knows a writer who bakes his poems into fortune cookies. My friend Alfred Lubrano is a newspaper reporter who turns his more personal work into short commentaries for National Public Radio. I know a writer who sold his poetry to a major athletic shoe company to use for their advertising.

8. Or consider the following.

The editors are right to reject your piece. When my novel didn't find a home the first time out, I initially believed something was wrong with the editors, not my novel. But I came to realize that *I* wouldn't have wanted to read that novel either. It was too long for my tastes, too somber, too vague. I preferred books that were tight, comic, specific. When I'd been writing the book, I hadn't cultivated my inner voice enough to know my own standards, let alone pay attention to them. It *should* have been rejected, because I needed to revise it into a different book, one that was more satisfying to me.

I also decided to become more savvy about the needs of the publishing industry. After all, publishing is a business. I can ignore that fact and blunder along, getting increasingly PO'd when my work doesn't find a home, or I can acknowledge that fact and be informed by it. This doesn't mean selling out or chucking all my integrity. It means studying the market and understanding, as best as I can, what it will bear that resembles what I can and want to do. Furthermore, it means writing well while mindful of these market considerations and seeing where and how my skills and interests overlap with the market. It's possible, as it was with the revision of my novel, that it isn't so awful to think about the market. It forced me to get my novel to a workable length and to make it a much more polished and exciting book—one that I myself liked a whole lot better.

In short, if you think, after a considerable amount of deliberation, that the editors were on target when they didn't accept you, then rewrite. You can do it immediately or years later.

In Sum

All the above is a lot of detail about the two fundamental principles of coping with rejection. And these are true no matter what, even if it's been years and you have never published a single word, and even if you have published seven books and can't get anywhere with the eighth:

1. Don't take rejection personally. It's about your work or their publishing needs, not about *you.*

2. Don't stop writing. If you love to write, keep writing. Rewrite the rejected piece or write something new. Just keep your pen on the paper. More than anything else I have said here, that will go the farthest toward keeping up your hope and faith.

THE WRITER IN BUSINESS

When you have been publishing awhile, you will begin to see that writing is a business, not only for editors and agents and book distributors and stores but for you as well. You are a businessperson in that you are creating an object that you are trying to sell and disseminate.

This is true whether you are striving to create the highest art or the most ordinary of pieces, whether you could care less about the size of your writing income or you are obsessed with making a million. When you send your work out into the world, you are entering the marketplace and engaging in commerce. You need to be aware of some basic rules of business that will make your efforts more likely to be effective.

1. Maintain excellent records of your submissions. Woe be unto the writer who is multiple-submitting manuscripts and keeps no records. When she gets her acceptance, how will she know whom to contact? What if, before she racks her brain enough to remember, she gets a second acceptance? She has inadvertently committed publishing adultery, and there can be no escape short of alienating one place or the other. All because she failed to keep records of what she was doing.

When I began submitting stories, I used index cards. I kept two sets, one for each story, listing all the magazines to which they'd been sent and the dates; and one for each magazine, listing all the stories that had gone there, as well as any editors' names I'd picked up from the rejection letters. You can now use your computer to keep your records, but however you do it, do it. You'll regret it if you don't.

2. Learn the phrasing of business correspondence. When you don't receive word on a story for a long time, write a polite and diplomatic letter asking about the status of your story, perhaps noting that you're concerned because sometimes your postal service isn't as efficient as you might like.

When you are multiple-submitting a story, say so in your letter. And when you receive an acceptance for a piece you multiple-submitted and need to withdraw it from the other places where it is being considered, don't say in your letter that your story has been snapped up by another magazine, and so you're withdrawing it. Simply say that you are withdrawing your story from consideration. No more is necessary.

That is, be succinct and careful. If you aren't used to writing such letters, you might want to look through a few reference books on business correspondence to learn how it's done. Remember: Be professional at all times. No editor wants to know he's dealing with a hothead or a whiner. You can be as irked or distressed or nervous as you need to be in private, but your business contacts should not see that. Remain dignified and becoming. Show others only your best.

3. Along those lines, be sure to observe the most oft-cited writer rules: Don't call an editor on the phone; don't neglect your SASE.

4. Send thank-you notes. This applies to anyone you meet for networking purposes (see "Networking" below), places that have hosted your readings, trusted readers, and anyone who has done you a good turn. Make them short and warm-hearted. I've spoken with more than one millionaire who said that thank-you notes were the single most important thing they began doing early in their careers—and they're still writing them.

5. Regularly keep up with all your business contacts—editors, readers, agents, anyone to whom you have sent a thank-you note. People are eager to follow writers' careers, if you invite them to do so. Send them new work and notices of your next reading or announcements of your latest success. (You might even want to maintain a mailing list so you'll have the addresses ready whenever you write or accomplish something new.) If the relationship is more personal, make a call now and then to touch base, especially if you find yourself visiting the city in which they are located. If you do nothing else, you might want to mail holiday cards every year, saying what you've been up to. Sure, it takes some time, but holiday cards can be good business; it is said that Jacqueline Susann's great success had a lot to do with the fact that her Christmas card list was seven thousand people strong.

6. Remain optimistic during down times. Remember that no business rockets right to the top, and some take many, many years to make a profit.

NETWORKING

We used to call it "meeting people in your field." Now we call it "networking." It is what we do when we connect with people who have an association with writing. A writer in your class. Your teacher. An agent you meet at a conference. The owner of a bookstore. The editor who is a cousin of your neighbor's father's ex-wife. The reporter covering your township meeting.

Networking is enormously valuable for you and the other people involved, and if you are at all gregarious, it can also be fun. Recently, an unpublished writer attended a literary event in a bookstore at which several authors and an agent spoke. After the agent was through, the aspiring writer came up to meet her, explaining that he was completing a novel and a screenplay. They discussed his work, she asked him to send her some manuscripts, and two weeks later she was representing him. Before that encounter, the young writer hadn't known any agents and had been wondering how to get one. As a result of that encounter (*and* the quality of the work he submitted to her), he landed an agent swiftly.

And that is just one story.

Networking happens at any time, with anyone who has any relation to writing. But, you may be wondering, that aspiring writer *knew* the agent was an agent. How can *I* figure out whom *I* should talk to?

Often the answer is obvious. The owner of a bookstore. An author at a conference.

But what about the cousin of the neighbor's father's ex-wife? Or a person at a party who, we might later learn, runs a writer's colony? How do we know who is connected to writing?

By letting others know that *we* are connected to writing. Maybe we offer that we love to write, or are reading a particular book we admire, or attended a recent appearance by John Updike. Whatever we say, we present a conversational opening to the other person so that she can add that her daughter loves to write, too, or that she took a writing class by the author of the book we're admiring, or that her brother is a major-league fan of John Updike's. Then we have a conversational thread to follow, which might, one way or another, lead us to meet or learn about people who are involved in writing.

I realize that some writers are uncomfortable with what they see as the moral dilemma of networking: They view networking as meeting people just to get somewhere—i.e., using people. Networking, however, is not about using people. It is about opening up your life to the lives of others who share your affection for writing and then mutually helping each other progress, both creatively and professionally, in your writing careers. This is the same thing you do with potential friends; in fact, networking is often no more than another word for making friends who share your writing interests. Indeed, you can even view it not as a social encounter that might lead to a networking opportunity but as a social encounter that might lead to a *social* opportunity. Because networking is a social interaction that focuses on your passion for writing and that, if you let it, can ultimately lead to writing opportunities.

The basic approach you need when it comes to networking is to be friendly and forthright. Ask questions about what the person does. Describe what you do and want to be doing. Offer your phone number. (Maybe carry a business card.) If possible, arrange to speak later.

I also always extend as much help as I can to the people I meet when networking. If they need to network into certain areas, I tell them I will speak to someone I know who is involved in those areas, and then I do. A few months ago, I met a writer who was looking for an agent who handles thrillers. I didn't know of any such agents, but I did know a romance writer who might. I gave the romance writer a call and learned that she did indeed know a thriller-oriented agent; then I passed the information along to the thriller writer.

With this approach, networking will indeed spread a net far and wide, connecting people who would otherwise never know each other. It's like matchmaking for business. And what fun it is to see if any of the "couples" I put together end up working out as successful business pairings.

You can maximize your chances for networking by going to places where writer-types are likely to be. This includes writing classes, conferences, colonies, readings, cafes where writers tend to cluster, parties thrown by writers. It includes any place where your writer intuition says to go.

I am not specifying a particular style for networking because it is as unique an interactional pattern as the way we approach new friendships (with which, as I've said, it has much in common). There is no script. But you will stand a chance of doing it well when you approach your networking opportunities with a sense of genuine enthusiasm and openness, curiosity and respect. (If you know the writer by reputation, you will improve your networking chances tenfold if you have already read his books, or at least some of his work, before you meet him.) And when you allow yourself to *be* yourself throughout the encounter.

If you feel uncomfortable talking to strangers, read books on mingling (which you can find in both the Business and Self-Help sections of your bookstore). But remember: The more you are your genuine self—the more you enter conversation by commenting on a piece of jewelry or turn of phrase that you *really* like, the more you sustain conversation by pursuing a topic in which you are *really* interested, and the more you express any positive feelings you *really* have toward the person—the easier networking will be, and the more of it you'll want to do.

AGENTS

When I give seminars, the question-and-answer period always includes numerous inquiries about agents. Although there are entire books devoted to getting an agent, I felt that I should review those questions here, so that you can get a good overview of the whole agent side of the business.

1. What is an agent? An agent is the person who handles your business. She reads your book manuscript to decide if it is marketable. If the decision is yes, then she sends the manuscript to editors who she feels are likely to appreciate your work. And if an editor makes an offer, your agent will negotiate to get you the best possible money, as well as negotiate the most remunerative deal on all subsidiary rights (which includes reprints, book clubs, dramatic rights, electronic rights, and foreign editions). This way, you don't have to spend your time figuring out who's who in the publishing world, and you don't have to face the potentially awkward task of negotiating your own fees. In fact, many authors feel that writers should *never* talk money with anyone in publishing except their agents.

2. How do agents get paid? Agents receive a certain percentage of all the money paid to the writer. For most agents, that is 15 percent, though for a few it is still 10 percent. Some agents will also request that you cover the costs of their duplicating.

A few agencies charge reading fees to look at your work. However, members of the Association of Authors' Representatives will not charge you. You can find AAR members by looking up the agent in *Literary Marketplace* (*LMP*) or *Guide to Literary Agents*, annual directories available in most libraries.

3. Whom does an agent work for? The agent works for you. Not for the editor. Essentially, agents are hired by you to do your business. They may be friendly with editors, but they are not editors, nor do they get paid by editors.

4. Are agents ever wrong? Sure. They work on the basis of instinct and prior experience. Sometimes circumstances change, or editors' tastes change.

5. How do you get an agent? The best way is to meet one directly. This is why it is important to attend conferences and parties. The second best way is to network, because even if no one you know has an agent, someone will know someone who has an agent. The third best way to get an agent is to write to one whose name you find in *LMP* or *Guide to Literary Agents.* This approach is particularly effective if you have done the following research: Look through books that are topically or stylistically similar to yours and see if agents are mentioned in the acknowledgments or dedication. Often they are. Then go to the *LMP* or *Guide to Literary Agents* to get the address of the acknowledged agent and send a query letter. Many people have found excellent representation this way.

6. What is the best time to get an agent? Agents prefer to be contacted by writers whose work is ready, or almost ready, to be submitted to editors. This means that you have a finished proposal for a book, or a novel that is substantially completed, or enough short stories to make up a collection. This isn't, however, a hard and fast rule; agents may also take you on when you have only an idea for a proposal, or a few chapters of a novel, or a handful of short stories.

7. Do agents edit your work? Most agents will make general, market-driven suggestions but do not make comments as detailed as line edits. Some agents will do more intensive editing, though that is the exception rather than the rule.

8. Besides book manuscripts and proposals, what kinds of work do agents handle? Many agents prefer not to submit stories, articles, and poetry, as the process is too time-consuming and costly, especially with pieces destined for low-paying markets. As a result, the general expectation is that agents send out only books, book proposals, and finished collections of stories, and let writers market their other work. This is not universally true, however; some agents do submit everything.

9. Is it a good or a bad idea to have an agent? For writers of books, I think agents are a very good idea. Not only do they have a better chance of selling your book than you do on your own, but they can arrange for subsidiary rights in areas you wouldn't have considered. My first book was sold to Italy for translation; one of the stories was sold to television and radio for adaptation; my novel was optioned for a movie. I could never have initiated these transactions on my own, let alone pulled them off successfully.

10. Can I end the relationship? First, try to work things out. Assess the situation: Is it you? Is it your agent? Is it the type of work you're submitting? Maybe you need to initiate a conversation about your concerns. If you have tried to work things out and feel the situation is hopeless, you might want to let the agent go. Often this can be done through a discussion in which you mutually agree to end the relationship.

11. What's the number one piece of advice you can give about dealing with agents? You need to trust that they are handling your business in the most effective way possible. You need not be best friends with them, but you do need to feel that they appreciate your work, want the best for you, and are doing everything they can on your behalf.

CHAPTER TEN

SUCCESS

Success. How we want it. Success is the distant paradise toward which we paddle, a destination we imagine will grant us happiness, even transform us. It is the brass ring, the gold ribbon, the *I-think-I-can*s blooming into *I did!* It is the Hallelujah Chorus of life.

At each stage in our writing development, we know all the fine lines and curves that make up the lovely face of success—but, of course, success's appearance keeps metamorphosing as our writing selves keep growing. When I was climbing out of a writer's block in my early twenties, success was getting one complete story onto paper. When I began my first writing class, it was hearing a hail of approval from my professor. Next was being accepted by a graduate school. On and on: winning an arts council fellowship, selling a book, getting reviewed by *The New York Times*. Et cetera.

This is true for all of us. What is universal to success is not the particular face of success—no one would say that success equals the Nobel Prize and nothing short of that will do—but the way that success feels, and how we can savor those feelings, and how, simply by virtue of being a milestone, success prompts change in and around us.

Because we all have different specifics for our individual ideas of success, this chapter uses the term "success" loosely. You may plug in your current conception of the term, recognizing that other readers will plug in other conceptions. This chapter is not about the nuts and bolts of how to become successful. It's about what success, in general, is; and what might happen, emotionally, socially, professionally, and creatively, when you achieve it.

But before we go on, I do want to address how to become successful, because it is such a frequently asked question, and because this most vital of concerns has the most simple of responses. To quote Benjamin Disraeli: "The secret of success is constancy to purpose."

That is, to become successful, keep on your path, using all your technical skills and emotional resources, learning more every day, focusing on your destination. If you tumble off the path, don't look at where you're falling, the tree you're about to hit; look back at the path, back at where you want to go, because then you will, by hook or by crook, get yourself back onto it. Keep this up long enough and consciously enough, and with some luck, you might well get there, wherever your particular there happens to be.

WHAT IS SUCCESS ANYWAY, AND HOW CAN WE SAVOR IT?

When it comes to defining success in general terms, we probably all agree that it is a favorable outcome of something attempted. Our friend Johnnie is attempting to get into Harvard, and he does indeed get into Harvard. We see that as a success. Or our Aunt Minnie is attempting to win first prize for the Garden of the Neighborhood contest, and then that bronze watering can does indeed get placed before her front gate. That is also a success.

Success, then, is when someone sets a goal and achieves it.

We associate success with positive feelings. Initially, a goal achieved makes us happy, exhilarated, possibly even ecstatic. As time goes on, the achieved goal comes to feel gratifying, a payoff for all our hard work. Other feelings we connect with success are relief, a boost to our confidence, an *Mmmm* of extended pleasure much like lowering oneself after a hectic day into a freshly made, queen-sized bed.

Beyond these fundamental understandings of success, however, many of us tend to add qualifiers, particularly when the success is our own. And this is why it sometimes becomes hard to appreciate the positive emotions of success.

For some of us, the qualifiers are that wealth or fame should result from the success. So while we all might agree that, say, publication of a book is a successful achievement, some of us might feel that publication—especially our own publication—isn't *really* a success unless it earns a record-breaking advance or gets us into *People* magazine. Thus, the happiness we would otherwise feel gets outweighed by disappointment. For others, success must involve continued career opportunities. Again, we might all agree that publication of a book is a successful achievement, but some of us may feel that our publication isn't *really* a success, and we can't really be happy, unless our book leads to a phone call from Steven Spielberg or an offer to teach at the University of Iowa. And I certainly know people who qualify success as that which will give them new social opportunities. They don't feel that publication (or an A from a teacher, or whatever act they're investing hope in) is *really* a success unless it leads to a deluge of erudite new friends and amorous suitors.

Clearly, the concept of success is layered and has an element of subjectivity. The base definition is the achievement of a goal. But on top of that we might add fantasies of the consequences of success. Hence, when we speak of success, we are usually speaking of two things: the achievement itself and the results of the achievement, whether or not those results are realistic.

Unfortunately, this dual definition can impede our ability to savor success. We can feel happy when we achieve the goal of, say, publishing our first book, but if we attach conditions (getting a call from the NEA, an interview on Jay Leno), and the conditions aren't met, our feelings of *Yahoo!* might devolve into feelings of *Big deal* or, even worse, disillusionment or anger.

Success unadulterated by fantasy feels good. Period. And those good feelings can go on for days, months, even a lifetime. But we cheat ourselves out of these good feelings if we make success too conditional, if we focus less on the act achieved than on the aftermath desired. Thus, if we keep shifting our emotional goalpost ("I'll feel successful when *that* happens"), success may always feel like a carrot on a stick, and we will never hit the payoff of simply enjoying success and feeling good.

So how can you hold onto the great feelings surrounding success?

Acknowledge each success (see "Celebration" in chapter three). Recognize that you need to stop and pat yourself on the back, that you have one more accomplishment on your life's resume than you had yesterday. Share your news with people who care about you. Give yourself permission to feel happy. Sure, new challenges still exist, but you need to give yourself some time for afterglow.

Success is part of the writing process. It is the final part, the period when we can bask in satisfaction. It is the sunlit gilt on city windows at the end of a hazy day, the *ole!* at the end of a vigorous dance, the big fat bonus at the end of an arduous year. If you neglect to acknowledge it, you will feel as if the finishing line to your current marathon is the starting gate of your next. Instead, stop, catch your breath, and let yourself cheer. It's necessary to celebrate success. It's human to shout *Yeehah!* It's okay to cartwheel, acceptable to grin. It doesn't mean you're not humble; it means you know there is a time for work and a time for kicking up your heels. And that is a wise and healthy thing to know.

THE DIFFICULTIES AND GIFTS OF SUCCESS

Success does not occur in a vacuum. When we achieve a writerly goal, we are altering our lives by creating something new and significant in the world, and hence our success sets off some kind of transition in ourselves and perhaps in others. Sometimes these transitions affect our social interactions, maybe in the way others treat us, maybe in the kinds of people we are drawn to or now find accessible. Sometimes the transitions shift the way we feel about ourselves or our work. But one way or another, success ushers in change.

If we are not prepared for these changes, they can be hard to accept. We might resist them, fighting to reclaim a status quo that our success has irrevocably tinkered with or already left behind. If, though, we are prepared for change—if we recognize that our changes are transformations that happen to most writers who experience success—then we can accept them and turn our attention toward the gifts that they have to offer.

This section is about what you might expect, both troublesome and magnificent, when you achieve a success that is recognized by others. Some of my observations will apply to you with only some of your successes; some, with all of your successes; some, never. My hope is that, once you see what might happen, you will sail through the tough stuff with ease so you can anticipate and enjoy the great.

Friends—the Tough Stuff

As you toil away on your writing, you envision all your friends and acquaintances and family being overjoyed at your success. You expect this whether that success is your first acceptance by a small magazine or the selection of your fifth novel for the National Book Award. How could your loved ones not be happy for you? You're supportive of their achievements. And they've read your work all along, encouraging you. What possible reaction could they have besides delight?

Most will indeed feel delighted and will embrace your successful accomplishments as they would embrace their own.

A few, though, may have a harder time with that. Maybe they would sell their soul *and* their grandmother to be writers, and your story in *The New Yorker* induces a dread that they might not be as developed, talented, lucky, untroubled, connected, mature, or nice as you. Or maybe they are exasperated that all their development, talent, luck, etc. have still not led to their getting published or published where they want. They are frightened by the same fright that once dogged you—that they can't, or aren't, or shouldn't and, in fact, that they won't.

Or perhaps they don't want to be writers at all, but they want to be . . . something. They have dreams, possibly distinct ("I want to be a radio disc jockey!" "I want to be Secretary of State!"); possibly vague ("Gee, I always thought I could do more in life than I have . . ."). And when you hand them a published story or new book, and they glance at your name on the cover, and they flip through the book and see page after page of words you wrote and someone admired and paid you for, they see the concrete symbol of a dream realized. Unless they are quite comfortable with themselves or are able to give their happiness for you greater weight than their own disappointment in themselves, your success may point out to them the dream they *haven't* realized.

In other words, you are encountering other people's envy. (See "Envy" in chapter two.)

I was astounded when this first happened to me. When my first book came out, most of my friends were supportive, throwing me parties, talking up the book to everyone they knew. But some friends who had read my stories voraciously—people whose loyalty I would never have questioned—began evading my eyes in the gym, on the street. They didn't buy the book, though it was the same book they'd loved in manuscript. They couldn't seem to make it to my readings. They acted as if my book wasn't happening.

Since then, I have encountered variations on this. I have an old friend from college who still has never acknowledged that I have published at all, much less three books—and this remains true even when she is talking about how much she loves to read. I have been asked out by men who buy my books but can't bring themselves to open the cover, or who don't even buy my books. (A tip to those who wish to seduce authors: Don't even think about it if you haven't read their books.) I have worked at a job where I had many pleasant conversations with an affable co-worker, who was herself an aspiring writer. But when I mentioned that I'd published a few books, she asked nothing about them or my life as a writer, and though she saw my books on my desk one day, pretended they were invisible, not even pausing to thumb through them.

Each of these experiences hurt at first, as does any major omission between people—a flattering dress that a husband doesn't comment on, a new baby that a friend doesn't ask about, a neck brace for a broken collarbone that co-workers ignore.

Then I realized that it wasn't me they were unable to face, but themselves. My books just made them think about all they hadn't done with their lives. If they dismissed my books, they could dismiss the nattering voice in their minds that said that they, too, could have been a contender, if only they had been able to vanquish their fears.

My success was their scapegoat. It didn't make *me* become different from *them*; it made *them* feel as if they were different from *me*.

Every time I encounter these reactions in others, I feel shocked all over again. Rejection stings, and when people don't acknowledge a very important part of our lives—particularly people we have trusted and liked—we interpret it as rejection. But in this case, it is not. We have nothing to do with these responses in people; their inability to recognize our success is a battle they are fighting with themselves.

If this happens to you, first, admit to yourself that you feel saddened by others' lack of acknowledgment. Second, accept that, as Natalie Goldberg writes in *Wild Mind*, success is different from love and simply will not lead to your getting all the attention you crave. Third, work on understanding that people's lack of acknowledgment is about *them*, not *you*. And then, turn your telescope away from those people and pivot it to concentrate instead on all the friends and acquaintances who *can* remain supportive. The others may come around later, when they have developed more of themselves and so are better able to dispense with their envy.

Friends—the Great Stuff

Each success is evidence of your growth—of your skills, your inner voice, your material, your discipline, and so forth. And as you grow, you will find that you carry yourself differently, gain entry into new places, attract a greater range of people, and so will widen and diversify your previous circle of friends. It's virtually inevitable.

Like: You write a story that is so damn terrific that when you debut it during open-mike night at your local cafe, people flock to you afterwards. Some just shake your hand; a few speak with you; and one or two—writers at your same level of expertise, people ready to see you as a peer—ask you out for coffee next week. Before you know it, they've become real friends.

Or: You get a piece accepted in a magazine. The editor who took it so adores your work that, when she's next in town, she takes you to lunch. You have a three-hour powwow about Jane Austen, the future of online magazines, and split infinitives. She flies back to her city of origin, you mail a thank-you note, and a month later you get a call from a writer's conference asking you to give a talk to them. How did they know your name? Oh, they say, we're on the advisory board of that magazine, and the editor spoke so highly of you, we just had to give you a call and see if you were available.

Or: You publish a book. You are giving interviews to all the newspapers in all your former hometowns. One journalist is so taken by your way with words and your outlook on life that she calls a week later with tickets to a play, and shortly thereafter you become romantically involved. Or the photographer who is sent to get a picture of you for the article spends all afternoon shooting, during which time he tells you about his idea for a book that combines words and photos. Later that year, you and he are collaborating on that book. Or the interview is for a magazine, not a newspaper, and the fact checker who calls to see if you really are a slender Columbia graduate turns out to be a friend of a friend. A few years later, you meet the fact checker at a party, and eventually you become his son's godparent.

My own examples of this phenomenon are too many to count. A man who judged a fellowship that I won, and who then sent a letter telling me how much he appreciated my work, is now one of my most loyal correspondents. A woman who runs events at a bookstore where I gave a reading rang me up a year later, told me about a bookstore that was looking for an events coordinator, and arranged for me to be interviewed, thus helping me land my current (wonderful) day job. Newspaper interviews have led to party invitations that have led to brainstorming dinners that have led to writing assignments that have led to theatrical adaptations that have led to more newspaper interviews that have led to close friendships.

There is no stopping it: Success triggers new associations with others, both personally and professionally, and the two are often intertwined. Indeed, at this point, much of my social life has sprouted from my professional life and, to a lesser extent, vice versa.

Of course, success can also enhance our connections with people we already know. Our long-established friends, who over the years have read our work and supported us through our writerly thick and thin, will have come to know all the back roads of our soul, and so we might find that the trust between us is now more solid and runs much deeper than before. And our long-established acquaintances, who over the years have read our work as they watched our successes mount up, might find that they have more in common with us and more respect for us than they'd realized, and hence approach us with the desire to shed the skin of acquaintance and become a friend.

Success may throw a few typos into our social life, but if we relegate envy to the margins and assign new and enhanced relationships to center page, it can also be a source of great delight, giving us unlimited opportunities to expand.

The Public—the Tough Stuff

Some people are starstruck. If they caught a glimpse of Liz Taylor pulling up in a limousine a block away, they'd be at the edge of the red carpet, thrusting out a napkin for an autograph, before poor Liz had a chance to exit the car. Other people are not so much struck by a star as inclined to throw muck at a star. Give them Prince Charles or our current president, and they'd have their vituperation ready, their scowls well practiced, their tomatoes rotten and close by.

Which means that, for either sort of person, a celebrity is either a deity on a pedestal or a target for ire or mockery. In both cases, that means that a celebrity is seen less as someone than as some*thing*. A name, not a life. An image, not a reality.

Of course, what it *really* means is that the people who are making such judgments are doing so out of a belief that all people are *not* created equal; that, on some level, others are better than or inferior to them.

Most writers do not feel like celebrities, even the more famous ones. Rarely do their faces grace vodka ads or national monuments. Seldom do their awards get mentioned in the newspaper. Writers almost never write while draped in mink and diamonds. Most of the time, they shuffle from desk to refrigerator to desk to library, their hair askew, their clothes wrinkled, their minds vacillating between charged and soggy. They don't feel famous or prominent. They feel like coal workers, or short-order cooks—people who roll up their sleeves and really *work*.

But some people in the public believe otherwise. A published writer, they are sure, is indeed a celebrity, and as such becomes someone who should get all the respect—or disrespect—which they always give to celebrities.

Examples of this abound. I'll start with disrespect.

A local newspaper put out a book review quarterly that featured two regionally affiliated authors on the cover, both of whom had written dazzling first books. The next week, a reader wrote a letter to the editor that said, "So you finally pay attention to literature. Then why waste your space on some nobody no-talents?"

My first published editorial received this response: A reader clipped it, circled what she believed to be my grammatical mistakes (which were, in fact, not mistakes), and sent it back sans comments.

The author of an extremely well received and popular humor book found that a columnist from her hometown had begun a crusade to condemn her writing and malign her character. (They had met once, fleetingly, at a large party, where their two-minute conversation had seemed innocuous.) The columnist wrote several nasty pieces about the humor writer, tracking (and bashing) her successes from book publication to talk-show interviewee to staff writer for a top-ten television show. Finally, the columnist turned her attention to other prey, finding some other dumping ground for her rampant negativity.

And for years I have been haunted by this memory: I once attended a reading by a lively and sensitive author who had written a book on how to find a husband. During the question-and-answer period, a man raised his hand and said, "Why should anyone listen to you? No one's going to marry you. You look like a pig."

Then there are the examples of being put on a pedestal.

The author of two novels finds that, at every reading, she gets at least one fan who gazes at her with stars in his eyes. (Possibly because she is heterosexual and writes about sexuality, almost always this fan is a he.) Throughout the reading he will be rapt, smiling. At the end he will come up for an autograph, then linger, perhaps asking writing questions. He will laugh excessively at her most minor stabs at humor. He will offer to get her water. As she's leaving, he will often try to ask her out but will phrase the question in a self-effacing way, such as, "I'm sure you wouldn't want to have dinner with me, so I won't ask for your number, but here's mine, in case you're ever bored or need something to do."

A newspaper columnist in a small midwestern city routinely gets piles of fan letters from women who beg him to marry them. Before he met his wife, he actually tried to date a few of these fans but found they were so intent on gazing in wonder at him—and, in some cases, trying to impress him with their own writing or get agents' and editors' names from him—that he couldn't bring himself to reveal his vulnerabilities. Needless to say, these dates went sour pretty fast.

The public is unpredictable. Therefore, when we deal with the public, we may encounter actions that communicate *You suck*, and we may encounter actions that communicate *You're my hero*. Of course, deification is easier to handle than denigration, because praise is always more pleasant to receive than criticism. But both are distancing behaviors that prevent us from being seen as regular people, and hence both bar our entry into real interaction.

This is how I've learned to handle negative objectifying: I see myself as serving a public purpose. Some people are so insecure that they need to feel that others are lower than they. Better that those insecure people should hurl their hostility at a "celebrity" than at their family or friends. (Which may not be the case, but I can hope that it is.) As long as I remember that the Rachel Simon they are attacking or taunting is just any old public person—not the me I am in private, nor the me I am inside—then I am fine.

My approach to being held up too high is to accept that I cannot, under the present circumstances, have a real interaction with this person, that their feelings about themselves preclude such a possibility. Instead, I try to feel sympathy for them. They think others are "better" than they. I, too, have felt similarly at other times in my life. Maybe eventually they will be able to sit down to a cup of coffee with me, but not now. I can stay in touch with them, send them notices of my next reading, but if I want to visit with someone who sees himself as my equal, I'll have to look elsewhere for now.

The Public—the Great Stuff

Most of the public finds success quite attractive. When you're a writer, some of these people are drawn to explore your work. Sometimes, then, they become fans who follow your career, popping up every time you publish something, letting you know how they liked the last piece, happily ready to read more. Sometimes they become more than fans, entering the realm of friends or business contacts and come around not every few years, but whenever the two of you want.

Whether they become fans or friends, the best part about dealing with the public is that it can give you a tremendous sense of meaning in your life. Through your work, you are letting others live lives and feel touched in ways that they haven't experienced before, augmenting their understanding of humanity, introducing a new concatenation of emotions into their hearts, designing new patterns of philosophy and wisdom in their minds, helping them drink all the more deeply of life.

That is, you are doing good. And doing good, if you are at all a sensitive person, also feels good.

This is the sweetest and most profound gift that success can bring you.

The following is one of my favorite examples. I was giving a reading at a bookstore far away from where I live. I had done a lot of publicity beforehand—interviews in all the local papers, on the radio. The audience at the store was sizable, and at the end of the reading many people came up to me. One was a young man who had smiled all through the reading. He handed me an envelope and, in a halting voice that revealed a severe impediment of some kind, he said, "Please read this. It will explain." That night, I read his letter. A few years before, he wrote, he had been horsing around on a roof, drunk and stupid, when he had lost his footing and fallen four stories to the ground. The resulting brain damage left him with not just speech problems but also physical disabilities. He had been trying to recover ever since, struggling against feelings of despair, and when he had come across my interviews, in which I spoke about my protagonist (a healer), he found himself feeling hope. He read my novel before my appearance, and the boost it gave to his spirits inspired him to work harder at his recovery, eventually leading—a year later—to his becoming a counselor for troubled teens. He still writes me once a year, letting me know of his progress, which is considerable. I feel blessed to have been such a catalyst for someone's growth; he jokingly calls me his angel.

A similar situation occurred at a reading of a first-time novelist I know. A bed-and-breakfast at the shore put him up for a weekend in exchange for his giving a literary reading on Sunday afternoon. One of the couples staying at the bed-and-breakfast that weekend was a husband and wife celebrating their fifteenth anniversary. The wife was clearly coping with cancer; a scarf covered her head, and she made several references to stays in a hospital. At the novelist's appearance, he read a section from his book that was joyous, a celebration of life. When he finished, the couple was smiling so intensely, they were crying. "Your hope is a gift," they said, coming up to him, "the perfect ending for our anniversary weekend." The novelist never knew what became of this couple, but he did know that, at a crucial time in their lives, he gave them some happiness and a moment when they felt a sense of peace.

Other examples: A poet periodically appears in schools to speak to kids about writing, and sometimes she hears back from them years later, after they have published their first story, explaining that her appearance made them decide to go into writing as a career. The author of a comic novel about divorce received a letter saying that her book helped the fan get through the low points in her own divorce and "taught me that I could keep laughing, even with all the pain." The author of a memoir about child abuse was approached by a young woman at a restaurant and told, "Your book showed me that I wasn't alone, that someone else had the same problems and came out just fine. It gave me strength. Thank you."

We all have stories of authors and books that altered our lives, helping us grow in crucial and lasting ways. In fact, it is often those very authors and their books that convinced us to go into writing in the first place.

That's the great stuff about dealing with the public. You are helping others. You are changing lives. You are making a positive difference in the world.

And, for all you know, you may be doing it for thousands of people, and your influence may be felt for a long time to come. Not much in life feels as rewarding as this.

Reading—the Tough Stuff

Ah, books. What pleasures they brought you as a child. Maybe you were one of the many who lived for those halcyon moments under the covers with your flashlight. Or, like me, you couldn't bear to watch TV or eat lunch unless you had a book propped up before you. Maybe as a teenager, you were captivated by Nancy Drew, Huckleberry Finn, Kurt Vonnegut, Rimbaud. Maybe you lugged books everywhere you went. Books were your potato chips—you couldn't stop at just one. You could read and read until you were full, and then you just wanted to read more.

But sometimes, when we become writers, we find that we do not lose ourselves in books as we once did. Instead, when we read, we are working.

This happens for many reasons. As discussed in "Whom and How to Read" in chapter five, writers often read in a quest for technical insight and so may be scrutinizing the pages to ferret out new approaches to, say, characterization. Or, since writers frequently pick up a book after editing their own work, they may automatically "edit" their reading material. At times, writers read to gain an understanding of the market. At times, writers read to review a book. At times, writers read because the book was written by someone they know.

Whatever the reason, you might find that, after you have begun to publish, reading seems to lose some of its ability to mesmerize you. Instead of charging through a book, forgetting your body, the time, even your own name, you may read consciously, deliberately, and critically.

Indeed, I know some writers who can no longer finish a book with a wholehearted "I loved it!" Instead, they finish with the more considered "There were elements that I enjoyed, and others that fell short." Or, "This is very well (or poorly) written." That is, the emotional response that guided them in the past has now been tempered by analysis.

A writer who has published three novels has confided to me that she is a bit ashamed that she can no longer read merely for fun. Often, she says, she hides her diminished enthusiasm from others, and so when interviewers or students ask her to name her favorite books, she replies by instead listing books she has admired. "I don't *like* books the way I did before," she admits. "Now, I *appreciate* them."

I can't give you a magic cure for this dilemma. But I can make a few suggestions that might help you get a little closer to reading with the sense of pleasure you used to have as a kid.

1. Recognize that, while enthusiasm can droop, it can also blossom. You may read hypercritically when you are in the thick of writing, but after your story/book is done, you may be able to send your critic on sabbatical, at least for a while.

2. Try reading authors who are deceased. Better yet, read authors who wrote in a different time period and/or culture. Then you are less likely to compare yourself.

3. Read a kind of writing you do not write. When I am writing fiction, much of my reading is in journalism. When I am writing nonfiction, much of my reading is in fiction.

4. Accept your reduced enthusiasm as you accept your reduced ability to run up ten flights of stairs.

5. Read when you're sleepy, especially if it's books you want to like (rather than "appreciate"). That way you will be less inclined to examine the words and much more inclined to sink deep into them.

6. Read books by people you don't know, for no other reason than that they look appealing. I have a friend who, once a month, buys a book by an author he doesn't know. He does this by browsing or by asking for suggestions from booksellers.

7. Join a book discussion group. If the group consists of people who are not writers, you will find yourself surrounded by people who have retained the reading enthusiasm of their youth, and so you might be better able to reclaim your own.

Reading—the Great Stuff

Of course, now that you can read with the eyes of a writer, you can see much more in any piece of writing than you could before. Whether or not you are grappling with the issue of reading more consciously, you will find that the entire reading experience has broadened and deepened for you.

That is, reading becomes not just what it once was—a journey through the text—but also an exploration of the process the writer used to get to this text. This includes both technical and emotional challenges. So as you read Vladimir Nabokov's *Lolita*, you begin to see more than a lecherous narrator, a sexual prodigy, and dazzling language. You also see the many strata of revision that Nabokov needed to reach this point, the reasons he decided to have humor here and pathos there, the psychological strength he had in pulling such a creation together. You see not just the *what* but also, to an extent that becomes greater the more you write, the *how*.

Indeed, when you read after you have achieved success as a writer, you may even feel a sense of camaraderie with other authors, since you understand much better than a nonwriter the hard work and patience and egolessness that was involved in getting the book done. Thus, you may well find that when you read, you are in effect holding hands with all writers, whether they be your contemporaries or your literary ancestors. That, in turn, will help you feel like one of a tribe, so that the next time when you feel alone as you're trying to overcome a technical or emotional literary challenge, you will recognize that many other people have struggled with exactly the same issues. You'll have role models to which you can turn for insight, and the security that comes from knowing that, though you sit by yourself to write, you are not and can never be really alone when you are a writer.

Writing—the Tough Stuff

The writing process follows a cycle: starting, revising, finishing, and starting again. But sometimes, when we have completed a successful piece of writing, we find we are unable to start again. Maybe we worked so long on the successful story that now, whenever we think about writing a new one, our thoughts pour back into the structure of the previous piece. Or we can't even get new ideas; all we can do is think of slight variations on the successful one. Or our present content is the same as our past content. Or our present themes are precisely the themes we wrote before.

Our successful story has gone from first draft to final draft to publication to precedent. It is now the established format. It has become our standard.

And we can't seem to move beyond it.

There are several reasons this phenomenon occurs. One of the most obvious is that, since the successful story was, after all, successful, our fears prevent us from being able to experiment with anything that might risk our losing that success. We may want to try something new, but doubt we could or *should*. (A writer sold his first novel to Hollywood for a huge amount of money, and the resulting film made a fortune. For months he was assaulted by calls from all his supporters in the book and film industries: "Write another book just like this one!" After pondering this statement for a while, he concluded that these people wanted him to write the *exact same book*. Which, in practice, meant he couldn't write at all.)

Another reason for this phenomenon is that we fear we have only one story inside us. This kind of thinking derives from the common sentiment that everyone has a book inside him, which we sometimes interpret to mean that we each have one perfect shaping of our experiences into one piece of writing. Although this is as fatuous as the myth that each of us has one true love with whom we are a perfect fit or the myth that there is a single political leader who will deliver our country from poverty and crime, we sometimes believe it's true. Yes, we must have only one story inside us. How could anything that worked so well not represent the apex of our being? We toiled until we found the true realization of our spirit on the page; how could it be surpassed?

Sometimes, though, the reasons behind why we can't move beyond a work we've already written are less grandiose and more everyday. We feel used up, tapped out, or tired. Old. We feel we failed, even with our success. We feel we were frauds who managed to pull off *that one piece*, but if we do anything else, our sham will become blindingly apparent. We feel we said all we have to say. We feel too smart for our own good. We feel too dumb.

Always, the inability to move beyond the prototype of a successful work comes from forgetting (or trying to forget) that humans are dynamic, not static, beings. We ignore the fundamental truth that change is the only constant in our lives. We fear the stamp of the successful idea because we fear we can't—or shouldn't—change. We don't trust that change will occur no matter what we do; that the successful story *can't* keep its hold over us unless we work very hard to let it.

These are the ways I have found to handle this dilemma.

1. Throw up your hands and keep writing the same piece or slight variations thereof. You can try to sell them and possibly succeed. Some audiences truly want to read the same work over and over, with

few changes. If this is the case with your audience, see if you can live with it. If you can, you'll be fine. If you can't, or your audience demands variety, then follow one of these other suggestions.

2. Keep writing the same piece, but let your work pile up until, by slow incremental changes in successive drafts, you inch into a new model and, consequently, new challenges.

3. Keep certain elements but change others. Your successful story was an illustration of the tentativeness of youthful intimacy, focusing on a girl and a boy in a rowboat on a creek. Then try a piece about the tentativeness of *adult* intimacy. Or keep the youthful intimacy theme but focus on a pair of cousins running off to a clubhouse during a family reunion. Or keep the idea of the creek but change the theme to being about the battle of loneliness. That is, retain the content but change the theme, or retain the theme but change the content.

This approach applies to all elements of the story that have too strong a grip on you. Structure, voice, tone—whatever. Change one element while you leave others stable. Eventually you might feel bold enough to change several elements or all of them.

If you are in need of guidance, feel free to nab new ideas for content, theme, structure, etc., from other people's writing. Their example can become your key.

4. Stop writing fiction and switch for the time being to nonfiction or letters. The form will be so different, you won't be able to replicate your earlier pattern.

5. Stop writing completely. This is not necessarily a dangerous move. There is a value in mere living; the mold of the successful story may have become rigid because your life has become rigid. Live until you change; then reapproach writing, and your writing will change. Just be aware that when you start again, you may have to face those big issues of discipline, commitment, patience, tenacity, and so on all over again.

6. Write a very long letter that explains to posterity why this is your final piece of writing. Then you can eradicate all the demons from your system by exorcising them onto the page. You'll learn about yourself, possibly finding out what your problem is and what new content or theme is attracting you. At the very least, you'll be writing.

Writing—the Great Stuff

Remember when you last had a complete eye examination? The doctor checked your ability to discern color and distance and shapes, and then swiveled a binocularlike contraption—a phoroptor—around to your face so that you found yourself looking through a pair of lenses. "Is this blurry?" the doctor asked as you gazed into the room, and when you replied yes or no, a new pair of lenses dropped down. "Now, is this one any better for you?" On and on, the doctor trying one lens after another, until the strength of your vision could be definitively ascertained. You of course had no idea what any of these lenses meant in terms of your eyesight; all you knew was that with some, you saw the world as fuzz, with others you had greater clarity, and with one or two, you saw a sharpness that, after all the mush and cloudiness, was almost startling, and realized that you had found the lens that was the perfect match for you.

This is how writing feels to us after we have achieved success. When we were working on our successful project, we tried all kinds of lenses until we finally zeroed in on our sharpest and clearest take on the world. The result of all that effort is that now, after success, we know the one lens with which we can operate best, the one that fits us to perfection.

In other words, our success with writing has led to our success in recognizing our vision.

Each success, then, becomes not just a milestone for our career, social life, and sense of literary community but for our creative development as well. Success shows us the current culmination of our efforts to reshape all that makes us unique—the memories and dreams and skills that define each of us—into art. But success isn't simply a culmination. It also an opportunity to pause, a moment of rest and reflection, during which we can, if we desire, take stock of what we are able and want to do with our writing and determine where we wish to go from here.

We write, therefore we learn to see. But also, we wrote, therefore we honed how we see, and can hone our seeing that much further.

When I think of the role success plays in creative development, I am often reminded of something a Peace Corps volunteer once told me. In some of the sandiest parts of the Sahara, he explained, the roads are not defined by asphalt or fencing, but by a series of oil drums, each placed far apart from the other. Travellers steer their camels to an oil drum, then stop, mop their brows, and scan the horizon for the next oil drum. When they spy it they venture forth. They don't know where they will be going after they reach any one oil drum (and hence, horizon), but they do know that, as long as they keep making their way from one oil drum to the next, they will somehow keep going.

Each success is an oil drum. It is the end of one creative road, the spot that was as far as our eye could see. But it is also the place where we can collect ourselves, get a drink of water, and see new horizons that were beyond our scope before.

We can use success this way not only because it helps us know our vision better, but also because success reaffirms our confidence. We find that we are more courageous about setting out toward that next oil drum because we *know* that our skills and emotional resources are up to the task. We have already completed a major writing project, and so, when we step forward toward the next, we can usually do so with the faith that we will, one way or another, see it through to its end. We may not advance with any more speed or efficiency than we did when we were working on the successful project, but the fact of our success helps us rebut those fears that we can't pull it off, or figure it out, or stay on track, or learn what we need. Success helps fight the *can't*s because it has already proven to us that we can.

Aside from vision and confidence, success helps the creative side of writing because it introduces us to new experiences, people, and philosophies, and thus we might find that we have a greater range of material at our disposal. And we can always do more when our toolbox is larger. In addition, our writing success has put us in touch with many professional contacts that we didn't have before. Consequently, we might feel a little more certain than we once did that what we write will ultimately find a home, and this may help us write with less fear and more comfort.

In short, success in writing benefits our creative evolution because it enhances our eyes and strengthens our gut. Which means that, when we achieve success in writing, we're in the optimum position: We not only get what we want, we also get what we need.

ABOUT THE AUTHOR

Rachel Simon is the author of two books of fiction, *The Magic Touch* (Viking, 1994) and *Little Nightmares, Little Dreams* (Houghton Mifflin/ Seymour Lawrence, 1990). She has received numerous grants and awards, including three fellowships from the Pennsylvania Council on the Arts, a grant from the Ludwig Vogelstein Foundation, and the Charles B. Good Award for Distinguished Writing. Her work has been adapted for television and theater, and performed on National Public Radio's "Selected Shorts." Currently, Simon teaches creative writing at Bryn Mawr College, writes for the Commentary page of the *Philadelphia Inquirer*, and organizes events for a Princeton, New Jersey, bookstore.

INDEX